STAGED!

THE BIGGEST NAMES FROM THE EVENTS INDUSTRY GO LIVE

AF515959

Sapna Gupta Navneeth

with

Deepak Choudhary

Foreword

Subhash Ghai

Om Books International

First published in 2016 by

Om Books International

Corporate & Editorial Office
A-12, Sector 64, Noida 201 301
Uttar Pradesh, India
Phone: +91 120 477 4100
Email: editorial@ombooks.com
Website: www.ombooksinternational.com

Sales Office
107, Ansari Road, Darya Ganj,
New Delhi 110 002, India
Phone: +91 11 4000 9000
Fax: +91 11 2327 8091
Email: sales@ombooks.com
Website: www.ombooks.com

Text copyright © Deepak Choudhary 2016

ALL RIGHTS RESERVED. No part of this book may be reproduced or transmitted in any form by any means, electronic or mechanical, including photocopying and recording, or by any information storage and retrieval system, except as may be expressly permitted in writing by the publisher.

ISBN: 978-93-83202-11-9

Printed in India

10 9 8 7 6 5 4 3 2 1

With a decade in the field of live events, and a bird's-eye view from the show console at over 100 shows, SAPNA GUPTA NAVNEETH has the unique advantage of knowing the Live Events industry inside-out. Currently running a successful and award-winning content start-up, she has worked on content strategy and creatives for some of the biggest brands, thereby carving out a distinct space for herself in the sunrise industry of content creation and marketing. Her latest is a labour of love that brings her passion for events together with her eye for good content. She is of the firm belief that there is a story hidden in every experience, and *Staged!* is her endeavour to bring the most exciting stories from backstage alive.

As a first-generation entrepreneur passionate about education, DEEPAK CHOUDHARY has been instrumental in creating companies, working on funding strategies and diversified business opportunities for successful start-ups including EMDI Institute of Media & Communication and EVENTFAQS, all in a span of 12 years. Over the past three years at EVENT CAPITAL, India's premier Event IP company, he has continued to pursue his passion with the launch of The Edutainment Show and Awards, India's largest media, communication and design education show. He has also created/ partnered other iconic IPs like the Bike Festival of India, India Kids Fashion Week, India Football Forum and Big Boys Toys. Choudhary has a reputation of achieving consistent scale for all the businesses he is involved in, and is equipped with industry foresights and sharp business acumen. A leader in thoughts and action, he guides the team at EVENT CAPITAL to become the best in the game and successful in the process at each juncture.

CONTENTS

For

My father who taught me to listen more than I speak;
My mother who taught me belief and courage;
My brother who taught me how to laugh;
And my husband, guide and innovator, without whose insights into the industry,
this book would never have been possible.

Sapna Gupta Navneeth

For

Jimmy and Nowshir who have been my partners in crime;
Anant Rangaswami who showed me the direction at every step;
The event industry for supporting all my ideas;
All colleagues and friends who have been with me through the journey;
Alok Jalan who supported my vision
My mother, father, three kids and the biggest strength – my loveliest big family

Deepak Choudhary

Subhash Ghai: The Ultimate Showman

FOREWORD

The stage brings stories to life. I fell in love with the medium way back in 1991 and created the 3D stage show, 'Cinema Cinema' with 42 Bollywood stars and hundreds of musicians and dancers. Even as far back as then, we had horses and a real helicopter on stage at the NSCI (National Sports Club of India) stadium in Mumbai. It was the biggest entertainment show ever to be seen on stage up until then. Since then, the live entertainment industry has evolved and gone from strength to strength.

The journey has been magical and I am delighted to see it being documented for posterity. What makes *Staged!* special is that it captures incidents, stories and defining moments in the journey of live events, therefore capturing the 'reality' of the industry. I remember the years when organising a quality event was like banging your head against a brick wall! There were no suppliers with relevant experience, production manpower was borrowed from related industries and 'event thinking' was very hard to come by. But every new industry has its teething problems, and events picked up at a dizzying speed. I have always loved the live medium and believe that nothing can replace the sheer thrill of watching an idea come alive on stage. Being a glamorous, exciting and creative industry, events attracted a lot of people along the way who wanted to make a career of it. However, it was only a handful that managed to keep pace with it and deliver delightful experiences to audiences across the country. It is these very leaders whose views are captured in the ensuing chapters of this book.

Staged! doesn't just look at subjects and views in isolation; instead it captures the back-stories of the leaders featured in its pages. It is through knowing their backgrounds that a reader can deconstruct their motivations and their unique contribution to the industry. It is primarily because of their efforts that live events have become accessible to every Indian today. Events encompass several genres of entertainment and many areas of interest. There are events around music, art, dance, Bollywood, theatre, sports, business and so much more. However, the following chapters go beyond merely talking of the different types or interest areas that events are made for. Each chapter is designed to give the reader a comprehensive understanding of what it is like to *be* an event manager. That means knowing not just the types of events that there are, but knowing what their own strengths are best suited for within an agency set-up. It involves understanding what roles event creators play, how the business of events work, future trends, and most importantly what it takes to stand out in an industry that is getting increasingly competitive. With chapters on the role of creativity, managing celebrities, being a part of a global industry, sports, music, festivals and exhibitions, *Staged!* will equip readers with a working knowledge of events beyond what meets the eye.

In this age of technology, social media and heightened communication, audiences are open to learning new things, scratching beyond the surface, consuming niche content and then exchanging ideas and opinions. The current awareness of events as an industry is woefully low, and as a true reflection of the events industry today with a definite view of the future, I believe this is the right book for the right times.

Subhash Ghai
Chairman, Mukta Arts Ltd.
Founder and Chairman Whistling Woods International

Wiz Sabbas Joseph President EEMA – Event and Entertainment Management Association of India; Director – Wizcraft International Entertainment

EEMA And The Narrative Called INDIA

Here's to YOU, the Crazy Ones...
The misfits, rebels, trouble makers,
the round pegs in the square holes.
The ones who see things differently.

YOU are far from rules and
have no respect for status quo.

They can quote you, disagree with you, glorify or
vilify you,
But the only thing that they can't do is ignore YOU,
because you will change things.

You push the human race forward.

And while some may see YOU and me as the Crazy Ones, we see genius because the people who are crazy enough to think they can change the world are the ones who do!

*Here's to All of us, the Crazy Ones...the ones who think differently!**

*Adapted from an Apple commercial.

The event industry has evolved over the last three decades, much in tune with how the media and communication paradigm has changedin India.

Quick to adapt to a situation, grab an opportunity, wiggle our way in, creating a space for ourselves –we in the event industry embody the spirit of entrepreneurship in its truest sense. Success stories have been created with a simple idea, hard work, dedication, passion and perseverance against all odds.

You will learn about the legacy of some of the largest and most successful event companies in India, thanks to *Staged!* Many of them share how chance opportunities led to establishing businesses, which grouped together, have come to be recognised as the Event Management industry today.

In our first decade,we were engrossed, and rightly so, in educating the world about Event Management and offered our services, saying, 'We can manage your event better than you can.'

In the second decade, the industry having been recognised and defined, has been developing different service offerings — integrating services even while creating differentiation; at the same time, cornering part of the advertising and marketing pie. No surprises then that every advertising agency wants to create its own event agency or, easier still, ally with or buy one.

The next phase is already upon us — the 'Coming Together Phase', to realise our power of togetherness and find common cause; to showcase our power as a whole rather than as individual companies.

The Event and Entertainment Management Association of India (EEMA) was born of the belief that as an industry, more could be achieved by working together, compared to what individual companies would be able to achieve.

But already a decade has passed since those first thoughts of gaining 'industry' status were mooted. Today, much like the nation, we are wired to define what the next phase of the industry should be.

Event Management is unique. Its clientele includes brands, governments, individuals, families, associations, communities and cities; no other facet of the media and entertainment space can boast of this spectrum of clientele.

Event Management, as a service provider, is probably the only industry in the media and entertainment space that can (and will) become a client to related industries.

It is well established that Event IPs have the potential of becoming brands in themselves. And in pursuing IPs, event companies are becoming content providers to media, television and digital platforms. IP owners retain services of agencies in advertising, public relations, social media and creative shops, much like our clients do for their brands. It is important to recognise that the future is likely to be ruled by these experiential brands. Consumers in the future are more likely to remember brands that have won them over through engagement.

In a world over-simplified by technology and galvanised by speed, the only platforms that provide a human touch are experiential platforms and experiences. The event and activation industry inspires and fulfills this human emotion — the ultimate clincher for influence and purchase.

As India continues to evolve and change,the events and experiential industry needs to evolve faster. If we are to be relevant, we need to be a part of the narrative called INDIA. We need to embrace and breathe energy into our engagement with existing government initiatives and campaigns, providing them engagement and momentum through the Live Events platform.

We have Indian government initiatives in the areas of environment, digitisation, skilling,education, empowerment of women and youth and 'Make In India' as larger themes. It is time for the event industry to adapt these government-led initiatives and build its own story, looking at nation-development with a passion that other industries are forced to emulate.

If You can dream it…You can do it!

If We can imagine it…We can do it!

At EEMA, the industry's apex body, we are leading by example, not sitting back or waiting for change to take place. We are identifying opportunities to work with and alongside Government, to recommend policy changes that usher in a modern, young India in sync with the emerging world order.

Let's not ask India what it can do for us (the event industry)!

Let's ask ourselves what we can do for India!

Let's Think Different.

Let's Be The Difference.

Vande Mataram!

Wiz Sabbas Joseph
President
EEMA – Event and Entertainment
Management Association of India
(2014-2018)

Deepak Choudhary, Serial Entrepreneur & Events Industry Enthusiast

AN IMPOSSIBLE VISION: EVENT EDUCATION, PUBLICATION AND THE ECOSYSTEM THAT SURROUNDS THE EVENT MANAGEMENT INDUSTRY

Heard of Narnaul? Likely not. That's where I'm from. It's a historical city in Haryana, about three hours from Delhi. Since there isn't much in Narnaul by way of infrastructure, I was sent to boarding school in Dehradun when I was all of four years old. From there, in a few years, I moved to Delhi and later to Indore before finally settling in Mumbai. In effect, I practically stepped out of the cradle and into continuously new and unfamiliar settings. As a result, I've always been comfortable meeting new people, building relationships, and getting things done in a variety of different settings. Maybe that's one reason people always expected me to be an event manager — to get things organised and 'run the show'.

I myself have always wanted to be involved in events. Two decades ago, that was a rare ambition. Not many people aspired to be event managers, and more importantly, none of the parents encouraged such ambitions. The live entertainment industry, while being real, exciting and tangible, has some pretty serious baggage to deal with when it comes to public perception. From the outside, it looks disorganised and fragmented. Despite extensive efforts to put a figure on the industry, we have no truly indicative number. It is true that it will take time to rein in the industry, put it in a structure and get every player organised! But it is still the only form of engaging consumers in real and tangible experiences, and I have always been determined to be a part of the system and be involved in its evolution.

THE ROAD NOT TAKEN

I had a strong entrepreneurial leaning, and realised pretty early on that the event management space was crowded. So, I set about figuring out how I could contribute to a rapidly crowding space, without getting lost in it. Eventually, I got involved in creating an ecosystem around this very promising industry; that included event publications, the talent system or event education, and the event intellectual property space.

I never had any doubt that the live industry was going to grow rapidly. A rapidly growing industry needs an ecosystem around it to support this growth as well as contribute to it and facilitate it. With this in mind, I decided to start by working on the hypothesis that a growing industry will need to be fed by talent if it has to sustain growth. So, my first endeavour in the industry was to try and build ***event education*** and provide a stream of informed and skilled talent to agencies. Being in a sunrise industry, I kept learning alongside the students, and soon realised that for talent to want to enter the industry, they need to know about it and aspire towards it. Similarly, for companies to attract the best talent, they need to be visible and communicate with talent. In fact, the entire industry needs to come together to first build 'category acceptance' of the industry and only then move on to build their individual brands. This led to my second major venture, which was to bring the industry together and create a platform for discussion and broadcast. I started an ***event publication platform*** called EVENTFAQS that had two *avataars* — online and a physical magazine. The vision was to give the industry a voice and a unified identity. After years of putting my all into these, I started evaluating ***entrepreneurship in the live events industry*** as a whole. I still wonder how much is enough? The industry is still estimated to be around INR 4000 crore. That really is a very small number when we look at the prospective playing field. Live event's close kin, exhibitions is already more than INR 20,000 crore industry. Weddings, another industry that is closely related to mainstream events, is certainly more than INR 50,000 crore as an industry. The burning question in my mind is — when are we going to expand the pie? Why are mainline event agencies not venturing into the lucrative exhibition or weddings space? The few that have tested the waters have beaten a hasty retreat. What is stopping us?

I had a strong entrepreneurial leaning, and realised pretty early on that the event management space was crowded. So, I set about figuring out how I could contribute to a rapidly crowding space, without getting lost in it. Eventually, I got involved in creating an ecosystem around this very promising industry; that included event publications, the talent system or event education, and the event intellectual property space.

EVENT EDUCATION

Let me start from the beginning. I was studying event management when I met several of the biggest names in the industry. It is very common for large agencies to approach event management colleges for students to help as trainees in large projects and events. This arrangement ensured that companies could identify good talent and make them a job offer when they finished their studies, and on the other hand, students too got to work on a live project and acquire practical training under the guidance of big industry names. I was a good student and so got sent on several such assignments.

My entrepreneurial ambitions had already started taking shape at this time. So, after a particularly successful large format fashion show in Kolkata, for which I was working under the guidance of Martin da Costa (CEO, Seventy Event Media Group), I candidly asked him if he would support me if I started off on my own in the industry. I will always remember his reassuring answer: 'Anything for you!'

It was at that time that I met Jimmy Nagdev Choudhary, a senior in college. She trusted my vision and came on board as a professional partner, and later became my life partner too! We were joined by another close friend, Nowshir Engineer, who gave the structure and depth to the idea and who came on board as partner. After that, there was no turning back. Before we knew it, we had the support of 40 big names from the industry for our maiden venture—EMDI (Event Management Development Institute). Since there was a large gap between the set of skills and knowledge that the current crop of students were emerging out of institutes with, and what the industry needed of them, we started with a simple formula — THEY (industry leaders) WILL TEACH, THEY TRAIN, THEY WILL HIRE. We ensured that only the most knowledgeable current set of event professionals taught our classes so that this need gap could be filled.

My entrepreneurial ambitions had already started taking shape at this time. So, after a particularly successful large format fashion show in Kolkata, for which I was working under the guidance of Martin da Costa (CEO, Seventy Event Media Group), I candidly asked him if he would support me if I started off on my own in the industry. I will always remember his reassuring answer: 'Anything for you!'

Today, it gives me immense joy to see that an idea I conceived 14 years ago has blossomed into a promising and trusted brand in education, now in the very competent hands of Sanjiv Chainani and Bela Desai (Greycells Education Ltd.) With courses across event management, wedding planning, advertising, public relations and digital marketing, the institute has spread its wings across four cities in India: Mumbai, Delhi, Indore and Bhopal. There is also a very large presence in Dubai.

BRINGING THE INDUSTRY TOGETHER

One of my most sincere mentors during the shaping of EMDI was Mr Anant Rangaswami, a man filled with ideas and vision for the communication industry. The creator of Brand Equity quiz, The War of the DJs and many more properties, Anant is currently the editor of 'Storyboard' (a much-followed advertising and brand show on television). Being a conscious innovator in the publication industry himself, he suggested creating a publication platform to bring the Events industry together. We followed his very compelling advice and started EVENTFAQS, which started as an online news portal on the industry, but has now evolved beyond being an online news platform, into an entity that brings together, celebrates, represents and rewards the entire industry. This growth has been spearheaded by two key people — Vishal Nagdev and Karishma Hundalani. While we were focusing on the education business, they were building EVENTFAQS. The platform subsequently went on to launch the WOW

Awards, arguably the most successful awards platform for the experiential industry. The latest endeavour is a growing platform that connects artists to brands called Entertainers' Connect. What started as a single offering called EVENTFAQS has now expanded to include two publications (*EXM – the Experiential Marketing Magazine* and *Excel — Experiential Celebrations*). There are three annual handbooks under the banner (EC — Entertainers Connect, ExV — Experiential Venues, and A — the A-list of event resources). EVENTFAQS also houses three event properties (The WOW Awards Asia, LQA — Live Quotient Awards and the MaxiMICE Conclave and Awards). Growth and lateral expansion are the only constants, and there are many more plans in the offing for the growing brand.

EVENT PROPERTIES

While these are initiatives that have made a difference to the industry, I still feel we are warming ourselves up for a big explosion — of ideas, of numbers and more. There is still a long way to go before this industry can grow to its true potential. There is still a large part of the ecosystem or support system that needs to be developed to enable growth. I was conscious of this need when Mr Alok Jalan (MD, Laqshya Media Group) started Event Capital with me, with a mission to support agencies in areas where they find themselves the weakest, namely finance, legal framework, media and digital competence.

Over the last few years, event IPs have emerged as a clear trend that promises to provide the next impetus to growth and longevity. However, the event IP business has so far been restricted to the larger agencies and big individual promoters because of the risk and expertise involved in making such properties successful and profitable. Event Capital was started with the mission to empower intellectual properties and help unique property ideas come to life from both a planning and business perspective.

Over the last few years, event IPs have emerged as a clear trend that promises to provide the next impetus to growth and longevity.

It has been just two years and we have had small but significant breakthroughs. We knew when we started that the industry had its weaknesses. Event agencies were and perhaps still are entrepreneur-driven. Agencies are run by individuals and their personalities, and as such, raising finances and securing a larger proportion of corporate marketing spends have never been the industry's forte. This is one of the things we have tried to change. We generate funds for IPs because no great idea should go to waste for want of funds. We have had small successes partnering with a few IPs. We have taken some satisfying strides via properties like the Edutainment Show (a multicity media and design exhibition, summit and awards), India Kids Fashion Week (the largest kids event in the country with Craft World Events), the Great Grover Wine Festival in Bangalore (the largest wine fest of South India with Invision and Vikram Shankar), the Bike Festival of India (with Rhiti Sports and MS Dhoni as brand ambassador), Big Boys Toys (a men's lifestyle expo in Mumbai and

Bangalore with Yes Expo and Laqshya Live Experiences), Manifest (the Founders Summit with Amith Prabhu), India Football Forum (with Sportzpower), Fulcrum Awards (a collabaration to honour excellence in Public Relations) and Kyoorius Design Yatra, with whom we have partnered to take the IP to Dubai.

WHEN WE TALK OF GROWTH AND EXPANSION, WHAT IS OUR YARDSTICK?

Size matters. Agencies may desire exponential growth, and the ecosystem around it may be conducive, but how far can this industry grow, and exactly how can we all drive growth? Consider the current Live Entertainment / Events industry scenario. The current industry size estimate is INR 4000 crore of projects handled by about 3000 registered entities. The top 10% of entities do 80% of the business. Which means 400 agencies or entities handle in excess of INR 3200 crore. Of these, the top 10%, which is about 40 entities handle INR 75 crore each on an average. The top five probably handle in excess of INR 100 crore each. Clearly the industry is top heavy.

The clear task to ensure industry stability and uniform growth is to see how we can expand the industry as a whole. Here are my thoughts on what can be done:

Option one: Make more agencies enter the '75-crore club', so we increase the number of top performing agencies from 40 to 400, or expand the creamy layer from 1% of a total to 10%.

Option two: Expand the average earning of the creamy layer from the current INR 75 crore per agency to INR 150 or 200 crore.

The current industry size estimate is INR 4000 crore of projects handled by about 3000 registered entities. The top 10% of entities do 80% of the business. Which means 400 agencies or entities handle in excess of INR 3200 crore. Of these, the top 10%, which is about 40 entities handle INR 75 crore each on an average. The top five probably handle in excess of INR 100 crore each. Clearly the industry is top heavy.

Whichever option we choose, we need to figure out where the extra business is to come from. It clearly can't come from the current pie, and I believe it does not need to. There are several avenues of growth on the peripheries that can be explored. Event entities and agencies do not need to cannibalise each others' business to be able to grow their own. For instance, why are agencies intent on managing particular brand stalls within large exhibitions; why doesn't anyone want to handle the overall superstructure of the exhibition? Possibly because it is outside the comfort area of what agencies and their vendors are familiar with. Again, why do agencies shy away from large format weddings, possibly because they take months to put together, and 'regular' brand business would suffer. Whatever the reason, there is a lot of business waiting to be captured just outside of the pie, and the industry has to find ways around difficulties to be able to catapult to an entire different and much bigger scale.

The most critical aspects of growth of a relatively new industry include cohesion between players, nurturing of talent, support to new players and fresh ideas, and finally administrative support. As an industry, we have been taking steps to consolidate ourselves under the banner of EEMA (Event and Entertainment Management Association) and present a unified front. I find the developments very encouraging, and my mind is constantly buzzing with ideas. I am confident that together with all the leaders featured in *Staged!*, we will soon see a bigger, more organised industry that will contribute to society and make life fun and meaningful.

Deepak Choudhary
Founder-Director, Event Capital
(A Laqshya Media Group Company)

Sapna Gupta Navneeth, author and industry professional

SO, WHAT EXACTLY DO YOU DO?

Only an event manager knows how difficult it is to answer the question: 'So, what do you do?' Let me try and put this in perspective. I typed 'What is event management?' on Google and got 444 million results in 30 seconds! Interestingly, when I typed — 'What is mathematics?', I got 159 million results in about as much time. This just goes to show that there are widely divergent views about what constitutes events, making it necessary to try and come up with a unified view of the industry. Let's try and put a finger on it.

This is a dynamic industry. Change is welcomed, if not celebrated! Critics of the industry, who complain about the unorganised nature of the sector, have to concede that it is for the very same reason that events have amongst the shortest turnaround time for projects. It is possible, and does often happen, that an agency gets a brief and is expected to execute the event in, well, less than a week! Having said that, while the possibility of a quick turn-around is an advantage that has seen many marketers through a crisis, it is not the desirable way of functioning. Large-scale events may take as much as a year to plan and execute to perfection.

THE HOTTEST NEW KID ON THE BLOCK

Branded Content is the new marketing mantra. Branded Content is when a brand brings a piece of entertainment or information to consumers that is of interest to them, and subtly places the brand along the way. So, instead of coming in the way of entertainment with a 30-second brand message, brands want to *be the entertainment*. They have started creating or aggregating content that consumers want to spend time with. The content is in line with the ethos of the brand. Some recent successful Branded Content examples are the 'Google Reunion' short film, the post-Wimbledon 'Jacob's Creek' Djokovic film and the *Johnson's Mother & Baby* book.

Branded Content is what the Live Events industry is about. In the FICCI Frames 2014 report titled 'The Stage is Set', Tarun Rai, CEO Worldwide Media, defined the business of events as BRANDED CONTENT FOR COMMUNITIES. To my mind the real difference between advertising and the live media is less about the size of the audience per communication, and more about the fact that live events have always had branded content as its backbone.

HOW TO EXPLAIN EVENTS TO A MARTIAN

Let us start at the very beginning.

Events are experiences.

The **Live Events industry** creates **Experiences *for Communities*.**

Any planned experience created for a group of people is an event. We have events that are branded and others that are social. Here is the whole, happy universe of events.

A METHOD TO THE MADNESS

All these event categories listed above comprise the Live Events industry. Reports vary on the size of the industry in India, but according to informed estimates, it is currently somewhere between INR 3500-4000 crore. This is just the organised part of the industry. The unorganised events sector is believed to be as big as the organised half.

With this, I believe we are still barely scratching the surface. These broad categories can be broken down further into more specific types, but the purpose of this section is to understand what truly lies at the heart of events, and this representation should suffice for that purpose.

A more methodical division of the types of events follows. Branded events can be broadly classified into three categories:

- Commissioned or Managed Events
- IP Events
- Experiential Marketing Campaigns or Brand Activations

Commissioned or Managed Events: In this kind of event, the concept, designs and all other creative output and content that can be classified as 'Intellectual Property', are the property of the client, to be used by them in future without any further payout to the agency.

Commissioned events are the 'bread and butter' of almost all agencies. In fact, a large number of agencies provide their services for ONLY this category. The reasons are obvious. It requires no personal investment on behalf of the agencies or their proprietors. An advance is obtained from the commissioning brand (client) and that is usually good enough to get the project off the ground. The understanding with all suppliers is that the balance will be paid to them on successful completion of the project and as soon as the client pays up, which is usually within a month or two.

IP Events are those where the IP or Intellectual Property either wholly or partially belongs to the agency. This format of events is usually annual (or at any rate, periodic) and involves relatively more risk than commissioned events because it takes a few years to break even and then start becoming a profitable venture. But once it does establish itself, it's proven to be a more sustainable form of business. Sunburn, NH7 Weekender, IIFA and Mahindra Blues are some of the well-known examples.

Experiential Marketing Campaigns or Brand Activations are events carried out at a location where the target consumer usually 'hangs out'. The event goes to the consumers at a time and location where they are expected to be receptive to the brand message. The events are typically small, with the interaction with each consumer restricted to under five minutes. These events are usually either mobile or held at different locations.

Definitions apart, I hear there will soon be more brands than there are words in the English language! This ever-increasing pie and practically non-existent entry barrier to entrepreneurship in this industry encourages the disproportionate mushrooming of event agencies every year. One of the prime reasons for employee attrition in agencies is that many employees who have got experience want to turn entrepreneur and start their own small outfits with almost no initial investment.

There will soon be more brands than there are words in the English language!

HERE ARE SOME NUMBERS TO SLEEP OVER...OR PERHAPS, LOSE SLEEP OVER!

Pool of Talent: India has the largest student population in the world, 315 million (according to a report by *The Times of India* in 2014)! Of this, a small fraction has chosen to specialise in the relatively new field of events. There are approximately 2000 fresh event graduates every single year, as estimated by Prof Ujjwal Kumar Chowdhury, presently Dean of Whistling Woods International School of Media & Communication, in Mumbai. And then there are people like me, who chose a career in events after doing a degree in Communication Management. The actual numbers according to Prof Chowdhury, are more like this: there are about 220 Post Graduate media and communication courses with roughly 50 students in each course. That makes it 11,000 graduates every year. All these fresh minds find a place in agencies or in-house positions in corporate and media houses.

The jury is still out on whether communication graduates or specialised events graduates make better Events industry freshers, but most insiders feel that event graduates only have an edge if their institute has very closely liaised with the industry, not just in terms of the occasional guest lecture, but in designing the actual curriculum as well.

DO ALL EVENT MANAGERS DO THE SAME THING?

Is there just one beast called the event manager?

Are there roles that are cast in stone, or are job roles in our industry evolving?

According to the E&Y-EEMA (Ernst & Young — Entertainment and Event Management Association) white paper, there were about 32 full service event agencies registered with the EEMA in 2012 with an average of 55 employees each. The same source says the unorganised sector is about double that of the organised half. The unorganised sector is much more fragmented and individuals handle far lesser chunks of business. That already makes the number of event managers (at least) more than double. Here is a representation of job roles in the industry.

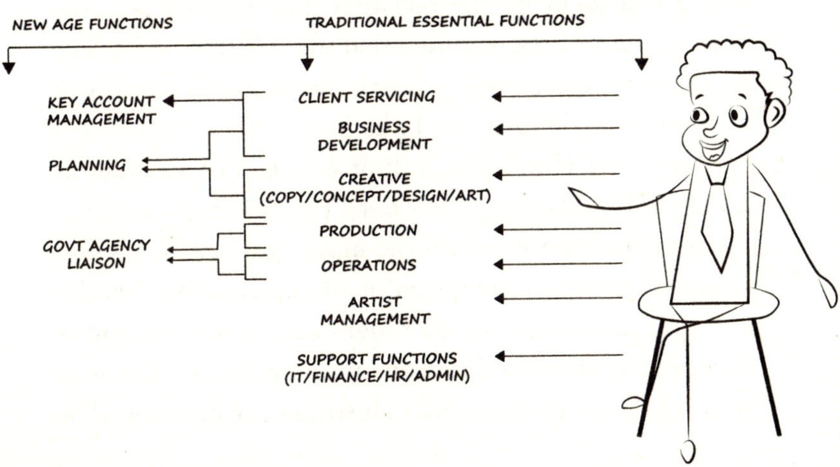

This apart, a huge number of professionals deal with one niche aspect of this service industry. So there are artist managers, artists, event content writers, set designers, specialised show directors, individuals who only handle registration processes at events and conferences...and so much more.

Here is how some of the sharpest young minds in the industry define their work:

Sushma Gaikwad, Vice President, EEMA-West and Director, Ice Global observes: 'Live events provide opportunities for brand experiences to come alive and that is the key differentiator for the experiential medium. The Live Event industry in India is growing at a phenomenal rate. The market has matured as events have made their way into media plans. The start-up phenomenon has impacted the industry. This entrepreneur surge has created pathways for skill development which has resulted in the birth of Event & Media institutes across the country. The event landscape in India has evolved over the past decade which is evident by the fact that governments are now taking notice of the potential that the industry offers. The Event and Experiential industry has been acknowledged as the sunrise industry in India.'

Karishma Hundalani, Editor & Head of Content at EVENTFAQS Media points out: 'Events / Experiences is the only medium in which the messenger can be present LIVE to ensure consumption of the message and receive real-time feedback. Another significant consideration is that the industry is a direct and prominent contributor to some of the most important industries in an economy. The hotel / hospitality industry is the biggest beneficiary of the event industry. When the event is offsite, the Tourism industry along with the Hospitality, Retail and Recreation industries of the host destination become partners.'

Says Gitikka Ganju Dhar, talkthestage, Live host and TV anchor: 'I am fortunate to be working in an industry that provides equal opportunities to both genders on the basis of skill, talent and professionalism. To a large extent, pay disparity does not exist. Though a bigger evil, the unsaid cap on a female artist's career span needs to be lifted if we want to keep pace with global trends. But all in all, it is a good time to be a part of the Indian Experiential Industry. We are all the builders of tomorrow. The inertia is palpable and EEMA (Event and Entertainment Management Association) is making a difference.'

The honest truth is that there is no way to define events that can do justice to the wonders that they truly are. As Oscar Wilde said well before we knew we were an industry: *'To define is to limit...'*

Sapna Gupta Navneeth

(L-R): Wiz Andre Timmins, Wiz Viraf Sarkari and Wiz Sabbas Joseph – Directors of Wizcraft International Entertainment

1

ALL THE WORLD'S OUR STAGE

With Andre Timmins, Sabbas Joseph & Viraf Sarkari
Wizcraft

Let's face it. Social media has changed the face of event management forever! If 'likes' were a currency, event managers would be millionaires. I mean imagine two consecutive news feeds on your Facebook timeline: one has your IIM (A) neighbour being awarded on stage in a business platform; in the other, your event manager cousin is standing between Buddy Guy and Nikki Hill at the Mahindra Blues Festival event, with the entire front row of business leaders staring in awe and ready to give their right arm to trade places with him. Which photo would you like (if you had only one like to spare)?

From rubbing shoulders with stars to trips abroad and experiences that money can't buy, the industry has its perks. Ask any youngster in an event agency what the best perk of the job is, and they'll tell you it's the chance to travel the world on the client's account. This also works the other way around, as an increasing number of foreigners now want to travel to India for reasons other than to ride on an elephant or see the proverbial snake charmer!

That brings us to the question: 'What does contemporary India have, to offer the world?'

A decade or so ago, the only answers would be Ayurveda, Yoga or the *Kama Sutra*. Today, perspectives have changed. India does not necessarily need to dig into history, culture and convention to wow the world. Instead it has many more modern, exciting derivatives like the cricket IPL, Bollywood entertainment and Sri Sri Ravi Shankar's Art of Living. The genesis of these now globally famous brands is traditional, but the final product for the world to see, gives a contemporary relevance to the traditional. As India continues to create modern brands that shine on the world stage, inspiration will continue to be drawn from the nation's heritage. Live entertainment is fundamental to India and a part of the heritage that goes back several millennia. And for this very reason, it makes for the perfect platform to take India to the world.

BEING GLOBAL IS BEYOND BEING INTERNATIONAL

There is a fine distinction between being 'international' and being 'global'. In India, there are over 3000 registered agencies that handle live events and entertainment. Of these, several agencies have planned and executed events across the world. Some even have small international branch offices. These agencies and the events they conduct abroad are international, but only few of those events meet global standards. A truly global event goes well beyond mere presence in countries outside of India; it stands for a standard that can match the best in the world.

The Events industry in India has long looked upon iconic global events like the Olympics opening ceremonies, the Cirque du Soleil and Tomorrowland as ideals that will take decades to create in India. But let us stop right there. Why does it all seem like a distant dream? To answer this, we must consider the Indian consumption scenario. Firstly, it is believed that Indians have a deep-rooted belief in value; we love to save money. So, a good deal works wonders for us, something that delivers 'value for money'. On any given weekend, an average Indian can watch a film in the best theatres for INR 350, have a good meal for INR 2000 and go to a nice theme park for INR 3000. Compared to this, good tickets for a high-quality live act like a concert or a musical will cost anything between INR 4000-20,000. In the Indian scenario, where we love to go out in numbers, with entire families, the cost of a live act can be prohibitive. The logic that the value of a live experience is worth the incremental money you spend on it, is yet to be accepted by the Indian consumer.

Secondly, the administration (quite understandably) promotes everything home-grown. Consequently, because of the tax structure and logistics, it isn't easy to get high quality international live acts down to India at costs that are viable for the consumer. The insightful first-movers amongst event agencies have identified the opportunity, with the result that we now have a few indigenous, international quality, live entertainment destinations like the Kingdom of Dreams (KoD) in Gurgaon and Kidzania in Mumbai. Going by the success and growth of these initiatives, sustained or permanent live entertainment is just about taking off in India.

Today, the Indian Events industry not only produces world-class shows for indigenous audiences, but also makes a mark with events in all the leading countries in the world. The industry has truly come of age and can compete not only in the traditional stronghold of story and creativity, but in technology and execution as well.

While exploring this subject, I met the three gentlemen who have in many ways moulded the structure of the Live Events industry as we see it today. They have also been at the forefront of taking India to the world. Here are excerpts from our very informative and interesting chat — where I learnt in a couple of hours, what would probably take me years in the workplace.

Wizcraft founders Sabbas Joseph, Andre Timmins and Viraf Sarkari are as different from each other as chalk and cheese! But what they seem to have in common is a TIRELESS passion for what they do. As I was escorted into what seemed like a small football field (but was actually Sabbas' cabin), I was temporarily blinded by all the glittering metal they have been awarded down the years. I quickly understood why they are popularly known as the big daddies of the industry.

In 1983, when Andre was 17, he started his career as a DJ on a salary of INR 700. About his initial days, Andre reminisces, 'I started my career as a DJ. I had finished school and my parents told me to go and work now! Being an Anglo-Indian, most people in the community were becoming waiters, some went to Dubai, which was a big draw at the time. I had considered Australia at the time, but ultimately I got a job in Take-Off, which is now Orchid Hotel.' Andre was from a musical family and so it came naturally to him. He played at Orchid Hotel where he met Viraf, who was a manager at the hotel. The two hit it off and began to make a success of the club. Soon they got talking and decided that since they were practically running the show themselves, they might as well open their own club. Along with another friend, they entered into a partnership with the owner of Horizon Hotel and started their first entrepreneurial venture together. There were four of them in it, and since everyone had to invest INR 1,25,000 in the new business, Andre sold his television set and video equipment, while Viraf had to break some financial bonds and take help from his father. The gutsy duo made a hit of Zanadu and soon made it the most happening place in town. Their club got visitors like Farah Khan, Salman Khan, Shah Rukh Khan and Akshay Kumar.

It was at this time that Sabbas came to interview them as a journalist from the daily *Mid-Day*. He was a journalist with a strong belief in social issues. He dealt with democratic rights violations and covered several landmark incidents like the Mumbai Police riots in 1982 and the Bhopal Gas Tragedy in 1984. While Sabbas was a journalist, he also had very deep roots in events and culture. Brought up in Mumbai as one of eight children, he grew up amidst Bandra Zonal competitions and the entire Catholic culture milieu. His father had a band called Joseph and the Jewels, which played at weddings of poor families to bring them joy and help make their special days memorable. All eight siblings played a musical instrument each, and the entire family would play outside their house every Sunday, with the entire neighbourhood gathering to watch them play. When Sabbas went on to pursue his studies at the Xavier Institute of Communications, he kept at his creative pursuits through the college theatre group and as the editor of the college magazine. He was also a part of the team that created the Malhar Festival as we see it today.

After the interview, one thing led to another, and Sabbas, Andre and Viraf started 'A to Z in Entertainment' together. Sabbas says, '1988 was about the time when we started looking at the events business. We had been around as friends for maybe two or three years by then.' Andre and Viraf decided to pack up their successful club business, and Sabbas his journalism, and together focus all their energies on the event business. Little did they know that it was the beginning of an industry rather than a business.

Andre and Viraf decided to pack up their successful club business, and Sabbas his journalism, and together focus all their energies on the event business. Little did they know that it was the beginning of an industry rather than a business.

GOBLINS, GIBLINS, WITCHCRAFT...

Today Viraf describes the Wizcraft business as more than the regular event agency. He remarks, 'With us what you will see is that we are not just about one area of specialisation, we are an entertainment conglomerate with multiple businesses.' The three (and a fourth partner who eventually dropped out) focused all their energies on their new event venture. In the process, they considered several names from Goblins to Witchcraft, before they finally agreed on Wizcraft — wizards in the craft of entertainment. Wizcraft was started with an investment of INR 7,500, with each of the three partners investing INR 2,500 each. The year was 1988 and Wizcraft started with party entertainment.

It was not just a big move, but one that completely capsized their current lifestyle. A very short while ago, they were swaying with the 'richie-riches' at their club Zanadu, but were now swaying on the Mumbai locals and buses, as the partners decided to give it all up to realise a dream. Their first big event property was called 'Conga Beats' which they did along with Lalit Modi who was then with Godfrey Phillips. They lost money on it and that is when their fourth partner dropped out. Through all the turbulence, their families believed in them, but they really could not understand why they all gave up well-paying jobs and ventures to start out in an industry that no one had heard of. To top it, they went on to lose money at an early stage. However, they kept the faith and gradually their business picked up. Viraf and Andre travelled on a near-broken-down Luna and undertook DJ assignments across the top-starred hotels. Through it all, the team started making valuable contacts. Soon, they landed a contract for an event with a prominent diamond merchant, and the rest, as they say, was history. They started handling large projects for entire business communities. They handled the birthday celebrations of both Mukesh and Anil Ambani's children, and Sabbas' wife, Punam, designed Mrs Tina Ambani's personal insignia. From birthday parties, the partners kept growing and started handling weddings and eventually corporate events.

MICHAEL JACKSON CHANGED MY LIFE

He did that to people. I remember Michael Jackson as being my first childhood crush. He changed the lives of a whole generation around the world, and ended up changing the lives of the three Wizcraft directors as well, though in a very different way.

Back in the 90s, international stars did not consider India a concert destination. Not even the smallest international stars ever considered India, let alone a superstar like Michael Jackson. But if there's one thing about Sabbas, Andre and Viraf, it is that they never think of the ordinary. At that time, if international concerts happened in Asia, the default options were Singapore and Hong Kong. Sabbas, Andre and Viraf were in no position to make demands, so they just began to make enquiries in the hope of landing a contract to bring an international artist of some repute to India for the first time ever. Andre recalls, 'When I was told Michael Jackson was keen on India, I thought it was a joke!' The star promised not to charge them a fee as long as they took care of his equipment and expenses. Such was their apprehension that Andre and Viraf flew across and met him.

'When I was told Michael Jackson was keen on India, I thought it was a joke!'

Wizcraft was just seven or eight domestic concerts old when they made this concert happen in 1996. However, there were several issues with the MJ concert as it was the first time anything as big as this was organised in India. The three lost a lot of money and almost went their separate ways. There were tense moments, but the partners stuck together and moved on. 'We lost our pants, but became household names. For us, it was everything; you couldn't put a figure on what this one event did for us as a brand,' adds Andre. Apart from what it did for the promoters, this landmark concert was the first step in putting the Indian Events industry on the world map. Andre's sentiments were echoed by Viraf: 'After this, international artists started looking at India for the first time as a serious concert market. Till date, it is the largest single artist concert that has happened here.'

THE STAGE HAS ALWAYS BEEN THE WORLD, NOT JUST INDIA

In today's scenario, the consumers' yardstick is never just India. With instant and ubiquitous access to talent, entertainment, information and even products, everything we consume is judged against its global competitors. The same is true of events. Every Indian has either experienced live entertainment in developed nations, or at least watched a video of it on the Internet. Indigenous events need to live up to these standards. Sabbas, Andre and Viraf recognised this very early on.

Setting international benchmarks for oneself always has its pitfalls. Sabbas says, 'There have been times when we have gone wrong, and lost a lot of money. But then we realised that we were too far ahead of our time and we moved out. In 2000, we started something called Catch-us-live', which was nothing but YouTube. We soon realised that the necessary bandwidth did not exist in India. So, we could not sustain it, we ran out of money.' It failed to take off, and the partners explain that it was much ahead of its time; audiences as well as the infrastructural support were just not ready for the idea as yet. For them, from the very beginning, it was about creating world-class ideas and experiences. Says Sabbas, 'We have done a lot of things with the global aspect in mind. We have brought Keanu Reeves to the Zee Cine Awards, we have had UB40 at Filmfare, got Deep Purple to India, Michael Jackson, Apache Indian and so many more.'

Over the last 25 years, Sabbas, Andre, Viraf and their teams have had several victories and some losses. All through, and indeed from the very beginning, they have had one shared perspective: 'The medium matters very little, the idea is to create a platform.' IIFA (International

Indian Film Academy Awards), GIMA (Global Indian Music Academy and Awards), KoD (Kingdom of Dreams) and events for brands, have been different media but with one shared objective of creating a platform — for people to engage with an idea, for India to reach out to the world and for brands to connect with their audiences. Here are a few of the platforms that were born in the directors' cabins, but played out across the world.

IIFA, GIMA AND THE IP BUSINESS

IIFA has turned into an insatiable monster that has left everyone in awe. With workshops, parties, premiers, business platforms and of course, awards, it is now a celebration of Indian cinema across multiple days that brings brands, stars, people and the media together. To give you an idea, here is what some world leaders had to say about IIFA coming to their countries, the various green initiatives and more:

'I'm very proud to say that Ontario had the honour of being the first North American location to host the IIFA in 2011.'—***Dalton James Patrick McGuinty, Jr (Premier of Ontario, Canada)***

'It is becoming increasingly apparent that India has a vitally important role to play in securing the future of our planet.'—***Prince Charles (Prince of Wales and Heir Apparent of Queen Elizabeth II)***

'...It is therefore very fitting that the UK and India are working together to promote Indian films, supporting and strengthening the film industries in both countries by bidding to host the IIFA in Yorkshire.'— ***Tony Blair (former Prime Minister of the United Kingdom)***

Viraf says of the trendsetter that IIFA has morphed into: 'For me, it's very flattering that we have an independent film star who tried to ape it, then you had a big media house who tried to ape it and a big television network too who followed suit. We, essentially a single event company, managed to hold our own and clearly stay ahead.'

More than a decade before IIFA became such a phenomenon, it was just an idea in the heads of Sabbas, Andre and Viraf. At the dawn of the millennium, Filmfare Awards was the largest film property in the country, and Femina Miss India was the most aspirational pageant for young girls wanting to enter the world of glamour. The partners handled both these IPs, but not as owners of the brand. Their experience with these IPs made them want to create their own on a large, global scale. They initially considered music because it was going global. But then, they realised that India has three religions — cricket, politics and cinema. Music was popular, but more as a subset of Bollywood than as a religion in itself. They knew that from the word go, they wanted to be a global platform. Sabbas says, 'We were very clear from day one that we had to be the best in the world. We never wanted to fight the Filmfare, Zee Cine Awards or any of the existing cinema platforms. We wanted to do something that was completely different and unique.'

What finally took shape was a Bollywood awards platform that was global. Says Andre, 'We wanted to change the paradigm, which is why we went through the trouble of creating a scenario where Dilip Kumarsaab presented an award to Sunil Duttsaab all the way in London, though they lived just two minutes from each other back home in Mumbai.'

'We were very clear from day one that we had to be the best in the world. We never wanted to fight the Filmfare, Zee Cine Awards or any of the existing cinema platforms. We wanted to do something that was completely different and unique.'

Sabbas added, 'We said from day one that India was going to be global. The richie-rich of the world are already emerging as Indians. If India is going to have a place in the world, IIFA should be announcing that, facilitating that, felicitating those who are achievers and at the same time heralding the arrival of India in the world.'

The first year was a daring attempt at this dream. For the first IIFA in 2000, they decided on London because it was at that time probably the largest Hindi film market outside India. Being the turn of the century, they decided to go all out and do it at the Millennium Dome. It was a time when Hindi films were not even screened in Leicester Square, so, organising a big event dedicated to Bollywood at the Dome was a difficult proposition. However, the real challenge was not to execute the event, but to get the support of the entire Indian film industry, who were understandably apprehensive about the idea. Says Sabbas, 'The industry was not sure how they would be received, whether people would come out to celebrate them, and whether they would be flown all the way there and treated the way they would like to be.' However, the Wizcraft directors got the support of Mr Yash Johar, who backed them and the idea to the hilt. The influencers in the industry slowly started getting swayed and eventually, names like Amitabh Bachchan, Ramesh Sippy, David Dhawan and more got involved and infused confidence in the event. Sabbas fondly remembers the legendary Dilip Kumar telling him, 'You all are mad to spend all this money, get me all the way down here and attempt an awards ceremony like this.' As it turned out, it was a bold move that paid off. As Dilip Kumar and Saira Banu stepped out of the car at the IIFA venue, amidst the lights, setup and paparazzi, all their apprehensions were put to rest. Sabbas added, 'He never thought that all this would really happen. That we could pull this off at the Millennium Dome. When he reached, and heard people shout his name, in a moment he was transformed and almost became 15 years younger. He said, "Saira, this is very good".' Coming from a legend like him, this was the ultimate compliment.

Clearly, the partners were looking at the big picture when they started out. As it stands today, IIFA facilitates international relations, promotes business and facilitates film financing, all while thrilling audiences both domestic and international. Such is the business generated by the event, that every year the biggest economies vie to host the IIFAs. Tourism is a USD 600 billion industry the world over, and over 50 million Indians are estimated to travel every year, contributing about USD 13 billion to the industry. Host nations see the potential of drawing the attention of these travellers to their country, and pay substantial amounts to IIFA in an attempt to win the bid and bring the event to their countries. The IIFA team works with the government in awarding the bid and makes it a point to not go to countries that have human rights violations or hostile relations with India.

IIFA is more than an awards event; it is a weekend of extravagant entertainment balanced with serious business. Between 500 and 550 media professionals cover the event, with a PR valuation of over USD 150 million globally. The TV programming of the event is produced and broadcast in over 100 countries, and is estimated to draw the attention of over 800 million people to the destination.

After the success of IIFA, the promoters are looking at developing GIMA, their music property with the same ideals in mind. Indian IPs have traditionally been owned by media houses, publications or channels, with agencies as creative and execution partners. Slowly, Indian events agency owners are showing the willingness to take the plunge, and become IP owners.

THE KINGDOM OF DREAMS

Permanent event destinations are dedicated venues where a particular event or live performance has periodic shows. So the same event or act is performed multiple times to different audiences. This has been popular internationally, and is a growing trend in India because of various reasons.

Firstly, it makes business sense in the long term because the promoters can create one show and milk it for all its worth over time. Secondly, there is room for quality improvement over time in addition to a higher initial investment; this allows for better quality production. Some of the most famous international long-term shows are the Cirque du Soleil and Broadway musicals.

Sabbas, Andre and Viraf decided to enter this space with the Kingdom of Dreams in Gurgaon. Like all things new, starting with the idea was not easy. The partners approached several state governments including Maharashtra, but not everyone could understand or go along with the idea. The plan finally took off when Haryana Urban Development Authority (HUDA), in Haryana immediately saw value in the idea and sanctioned nine acres of land for the project. Described by the promoters as 'a spectacle so grand, it can fit only in your dreams', it is an event destination that brings Bollywood-style live entertainment to audiences. It has a massive spread of 100,000 square feet.

To us, as an industry, it is more than an alternative entertainment option for the weekend; it is a live entertainment option at par with several international shows. As Viraf aptly puts it, 'We have invested over INR 300 crore in it and believe that this is a real showcase of India to the world. Some people see it as a real estate play, some as a theatre, but what it actually is, is retailing entertainment.' The promoters are very optimistic about the prospects. Initial numbers show that the Zangoora has had more than 1,300 shows and is still going strong. Several important people from the world of entertainment like the Chairman of Walt Disney, Steve Wynn and several chief ministers and heads of state, have attended its shows to understand the market and study KoD's success. The venue caters to about 15,000 customers a week and hopes to recover all the investment by the seventh year. The success of this venture has led many state Chief Ministers in the country to now offer land and support. Andre says,'The Kingdom of Dreams has opened several doors for us. We have been invited to set this up in Vegas and Shanghai. Dubai is setting up a Hollywood-Bollywood park and we have been invited to produce content for that too.'

'We have invested over INR 300 crore in it (Kingdom of Dreams) and believe that this is a real showcase of India to the world. Some people see it as a real estate play, some as a theatre, but what it actually is, is retailing entertainment.'

BRANDS AND THE GLOBAL VISION

The creation of IP events and other innovations like event destinations are long-term ideas. Often a high initial investment is required alongside tremendous vision and understanding of where industries and the country's administration are headed. As a consequence, these events and properties cannot be counted on to put food on the table or pay salaries in the immediate term. Corporate or commissioned shows are the bread and butter of the Events industry. The vision of corporate events can well be long term, especially in the case of annual events, but the biggest advantage is little or no investment and immediate payment.

It's a virtual battlefield out there in the corporate events space. There was a time when the battle was fought mostly on pricing, but like everything else, connectivity and global exposure have driven brand expectations sky-high. Creativity, quality execution and cutting edge technology have all got to be aced if an agency wants to be on top of the game. Sabbas, Andre and Viraf tackled this space with as much gusto as they did everything else. The result was that they emerged as a truly global brand in this sphere as well, something only a small handful of agencies have managed to do in India.

Sabbas, who spearheads this division said, 'The work that we do is very serious. Whether we use entertainers or not, it's all about quality. So, when Bill Gates came to India in 2007-2008, the first agency he looked at was us, and after that, almost every time he has come to India, Wizcraft has been the only agency that has managed him.' He continues to explain that the quality of management and execution was so professional that after every such visit, the Managing Director of Microsoft in India was promoted! The team has looked after and managed visits of many significant leaders including heads of Nokia, Michael Dell, Jack Welch and others.

The team has also planned and executed world-class events like the prestigious Tattoo event for the Sultanate of Oman, which is a music festival where the country's security forces perform. The pitch for the first Tattoo event was held amongst agencies across the world, and Sabbas, Andre and Viraf won the multi-agency pitch. The event took careful planning, and production took over a year. The agency also has the international mandate to handle virtually all of IBM's shows; they have handled shows for Royal Enfield in London, Birmingham, Manchester and Switzerland. This is apart from the events they handle for most of the top brands globally.

Sabbas explained that the reason they have been able to replicate their success across entertainment platforms is because of a single vision that brings all their silos together. 'We have tremendous experience working across the world. We also have tremendous experience in doing large projects but with great detail. The larger the project, the greater the detail required. Sometimes for small projects you need to bring that "large-format" thinking, and that is where we score.'

SOME DISTANCE TRAVELLED, SOME MORE TO GO

Events are much more than entertainment platforms, as far as the partners are concerned. They see events as a platform for change, progress and relationships. When S Jaishankar became the Foreign Secretary, he invited all the ambassadors from across the world, to Delhi for a conference that was also addressed by the Prime Minister. Sabbas was invited to speak on cultural diplomacy, a subject that has always driven him.

Through events, promotions, digital media, PR, and television production, the endeavour has always been global. Sabbas points out, 'There was a time when, being a journalist, I was very uncomfortable talking about money. Then came a time when we all developed the same skills. So, while each of us is still better at a particular aspect or function, anyone can do the other's thing if required. We have grown and evolved, so Wizcraft can today just be as it is with any one of us running it, or continue with all three of us running it. It can also make do with none of us at the helm. That's our dream. We have evolved and developed the organisation to the extent that it can do without us. And for us, that is the real story.'

Undoubtedly, the most exciting question in life is: 'What next?' So, what is next for the industry? Where can we take the Indian Event Management industry to? Let us not see events as just that, let us see it as part of culture, tourism, media and entertainment and as part of consumer behaviour itself. As an integrated whole.

Like I said earlier, the three directors started out to set up a business but unwittingly started off a whole industry. Our expectation is that while shaping the industry, they will end up liberalising the entertainment economy.

Anil Singh (L), Managing Director and Vivek Singh (R), Joint Managing Director, Procam International

2

SCORING WITH SPORTS

With Anil Singh & Vivek Singh, ***Procam International***

I suppose even the geeks and academic toppers will agree that as children, we always felt that the real stars in school were the sports stars. There was a small problem with this though. School-level sports stars in India lost their sheen rather quickly, when they realised that unless they made it big in cricket at the national level, they weren't going to be very rich.

Fortunately, things look like they may change very soon. The business of sport has evolved surely but steadily over the last few decades. There has been a dramatic rise in the scope of sports in India over the last few years. Currently, there are major sports leagues across at least 11 different sports, including some in the offing. Predictably, the wave started with cricket. The hugely successful Indian Premier League (IPL) started in 2008 by marrying cricket and entertainment to make sports a family entertainer for the first time. Even Bollywood seems to have taken a cue from this trend and films like *Chak De India* on hockey and *Mary Kom* on the boxing star are proving successful at the box office and are being widely talked about across media. There is suddenly money, respect and recognition in sports like hockey, badminton, kabaddi, athletics, football, etc.

Managing this rapidly growing sports industry is critical to ensure sustainability. A short-lived success story is not much of a win. A KPMG-CII (Confederation of Indian Industry) report, called Business of Sports, says that the global sports industry is worth approximately USD 600 billion, and covers allied businesses like sports manufacturing, retail, tourism, sports medicine, venues and infrastructure, media and hospitality, and merchandising. India does not yet have a comprehensive study that can put a figure to the size of the sports industry here, but it does seem to be growing rapidly.

From the point of view of events and live entertainment, sports events and sports marketing are rapidly growing segments of consumer engagement. India's recent successes in various sports in the international arena as well as the birth of various sports leagues have given the right impetus for growth. Some of the major sports promoters and sports management companies in India are Procam International, IMG Reliance, Nimbus Sport, Rhiti Sports and several others. Major sports marketing and sports management companies in India are focusing on:

Sporting Talent Management: This includes managing sports stars and their business deals. It includes their brand endorsement deals, media appearances, league dealing, etc.

Sponsorships or Sports Marketing: This primarily involves bringing in corporate funding for sporting events. It includes ways in which brands can engage with a sport and its consumers.

Sports IPs: This entails creating, promoting and sustaining every aspect of an Intellectual Property sports event.

Sports Promotions and Events: This includes marketing efforts around sporting events and properties.

Sports Venue Management: Managing a venue built for sports and handling not just events at the venue but parts of its marketing and upkeep as well.

I met the leading promoters of sports properties in the country, brothers Anil and Vivek Singh, to get their perspective on the sports management industry. Right away, I felt the brothers were as different as chalk and cheese. Vivek was soft spoken and sophisticated, while Anil was flamboyant, charismatic with a deep loud voice that fills the room. Both were disarmingly charming, and both virtual goldmines of insights and information about sports and entertainment in India.

Anil and Vivek Singh are promoters and proprietors of the leading leisure and sports management company — Procam International. The company is one of the oldest indigenous sports management companies of the country, with over 27 years in the business. The brothers have promoted an array of world-class sporting events, including India's premier running event — the Mumbai Marathon.

A CLEAN START

We discussed their upbringing and formative years to understand how they came about practically creating the sports management industry in India. The brothers were born and brought up in Mumbai. Their father was a prolific sportsman; a talented equestrian who was a trick rider and show jumper. He was in the Indian Army and commanded the 21st Mountain Regiment. He was also the National Steeplechase Champion. Their mother loved the outdoors as well and was very fond of riding. Clearly sports runs in their blood. The brothers played rugby and Anil was particularly good at it. He played rugby for India and was a national-level tennis champion as well.

A MARATHON BEGINS

It came as no surprise, therefore, when the brothers decided to convert their passion for sport into their profession. Vivek started off with sports right away, while Anil decided to take up a job with the Travel Corporation of India, though he changed tracks to sports very quickly. He recollected with a smile that his first salary was INR 450. He was given an annual target, which the well-connected youngster achieved four times over within two weeks of joining! Having suitably demonstrated that he was made for bigger things, Anil moved on to the sports industry only to discover that there wasn't one.

Anil and Vivek Singh were very much up to the challenge of making an industry where there was none. They moved from rugby tackles to tackling some pretty big challenges in the real world, in their endeavour to make sports management in India match up to international standards. Little wonder that Anil lost all his hair in the process and Vivek managed to hold on to just a few strands. What saw the brothers through was their belief in values and principles. While they have grown over the years, they have always chosen to expand their team by looking at qualities over qualifications.

HOW IT ALL BEGAN

When they started 26 years ago, the brothers' ideas and ideals were global, inspired by the London Marathon and the Wimbledon. They decided to bring that level of sports management to India, but it was no mean task. As Vivek added with a laugh, 'When we started off, people couldn't understand why.' There was really no concept of professionally managing sports events. When they organised their initial tennis tournaments, the brothers had to get marriage contractors and *pandal* decorators to work on setting up the event, because there was no industry and not a single supplier who had ever worked on a professional sports setup. Anil and Vivek found that they had to not just learn the ropes themselves, but had to 're-tune' and train suppliers and associates along the way.

It wasn't like there were no sporting events. There were several, but not organised in any significant manner. Like Vivek Singh put it, 'Sporting events existed out of the whims and fancies of the MD or the Chairman (of sponsor brands). So, if he made soap but liked golf, he sponsored golf — even if golf had no connect with soap.'

THE BEGINING OF THE FUTURE: SPORTS IP EVENTS

There are several aspects of sports management and marketing, some of which we listed out at the beginning of this chapter. Key amongst these is creating IP events, and that is really where Anil and Vivek Singh have been front-runners in India. Anil categorically states: 'We are promoters, not organisers. There is a big difference.' A promoter thinks through the idea, develops it, has a vision and is responsible for the entire ecosystem that surrounds it. An organiser, on the other hand, gets commissioned events, and goes on to plan and execute them to perfection. Promoters develop and own the idea and then invite brands to partner and align with the event. Promoters take the financial and organisational risk in-house on the strength of their belief and idea. Then they find creative means of offloading risk and making the idea profitable, through title sponsors, associate sponsors, television rights, and merchandising amongst other things.

SPORTS IPs IN INDIA THAT HAVE HAD A PODIUM FINISH

Today there are several examples of successful sports IPs in India. The cricket IPL (Indian Premier League) is foremost on most people's mind. Others are the Chennai Open Tennis owned by IMG (International Management Group), the Mumbai Marathon and Delhi Half Marathon owned by Procam International. Of late there have been several sports IPs created around sporting leagues, and the trend can only grow. Admittedly, with several hits there have been some misses too as far as sports IP events are concerned. F1 (Formula 1) motor racing came into India amidst a lot of talk and excitement, but is currently suspended.

Anil and Vivek Singh, Owners of Procam International and promoters of the very successful Mumbai Marathon and Delhi Half Marathon took me through the journey of creating that hugely successful IP, and it's a story well worth a read!

TAILOR MADE FOR INDIA

The Standard Chartered Mumbai Marathon, as it is called today, is an integral part of Mumbai's calendar, and preparations for it are on through the year. When Anil and Vivek thought of bringing distance running to India, the idea was not that India is a great running nation, and, therefore, a marathon is a good fit. The thought ran way deeper. As Anil puts it, 'All great cities in the world have marathons that they are qualified by. So, do we consider where we live, Mumbai, (referring back to the time when it all started), to be a great city at par with global big cities? The answer is "Yes", whichever way we want to look at it. If that is the case, we need a marathon!' With that considered, the challenge was to figure out how they could make that reality work within India or even Mumbai. So what does it take to get Mumbai out on the street and running. Clearly, talking about the health benefits of running may not be the answer. Everybody already knew that running was healthy, but still did not do it. Somehow, it was not reason or motivation enough to get the average Mumbaikar on their feet.

'All great cities in the world have marathons that they are qualified by. So, do we consider where we live, Mumbai, (referring back to the time when it all started), to be a great city at par with global big cities? The answer is "Yes", whichever way we want to look at it. If that is the case, we need a marathon!'

The big question was, 'How do we realise our vision and get Mumbai to be a part of a global story?' There are several small marathons all over the world and even all over our country, but what was needed was something that makes Indians connect with the idea. What resulted from all these deliberations was the 'Dream Run'. The Dream Run is one of the six categories that participants can contest in. It is a concept that exists only in India, and is a runaway success. It is what probably makes the Mumbai Marathon what it is. The Dream Run is over a 6-km stretch as opposed to 42 km for the full length Marathon and 21 km for the Half Marathon. The category suddenly made the race more inclusive and accessible. It wasn't just for professional runners any more, it was for all citizens who believed in it. It didn't take years of rigorous practice; some months of discipline and practice were good enough to give the Dream Run a shot. The charity angle is another resounding success for the IP. The Standard Chartered Mumbai Marathon is considered to be India's largest charity platform for non-profit organisations to raise funds. Causes range from arts, culture and sports development, to disability education, wildlife and much more. Now, you didn't even need to run to be a part of the marathon. Organisations register with the event's official charity partner to raise awareness and actual funds for a particular charity.

FROM THE DRAWING BOARD TO THE FIRE

Any event manager will tell you that it's one thing to ideate and plan, and quite another to execute the plan to the letter. In Anil's words, 'You take brand values, and you take management thinking, and the sponsor's global experiences (in this case Standard Chartered) and go to the people with an event they identify with.' It's a tough task because they not only decided to do something that is a first, but they decided to make it so big that big money was needed to pull it off. So it was a little bit of a chicken-and-egg situation. But that did not scare the promoters. They have always had a clear policy: 'If I believe in something, and I can see the method in the madness, then I'm open to all the methods in my madness being attacked, changed, chipped and maybe even dropped and rethought. But the main platform of the madness is there. We have faith in ourselves. If I know it's an idea, then I know I can find one person out there who thinks like me and will see this through with me. That is how I think we grow stories.'

Once the marathon started going live, the brothers realised that doing the marathon live was like another marathon in itself! The area or stretch where the action happens was not like a captive stadium where cameras could be fixed. Then there were other larger issues like where signals can bounce from for the live telecast. What it took was to shut down a large part of a very large city for a whole day and more. To do that, they had to work hard to change the mindset of every administrative department in the city. When they first requested the traffic commissioner to close streets down for a day, everyone was aghast. It took a 'Can do, Will do' attitude on their part to finally manage all the arrangements. Today, the administration sees value in the event. The Central and Western Railways actually start their trains as early as 3 am only during the Mumbai Marathon, without Procam even requesting them to. Today the distance running community and the business that has come out of it, including all aspects of sponsorships, coaching etc., is INR 800 crore. That is as close to cricket figures as any other sport has probably got.

Anil and Vivek's courage of conviction seems to have paid off as far as the Standard Chartered Mumbai Marathon is concerned. It is reportedly the largest marathon in Asia as well as the largest mass participating sporting event in the continent. It is also the richest race in India in terms of the prize pool. This is apart from it being one of the largest charity platforms as mentioned earlier. The Delhi Half Marathon is another distance running success story for them, being the world's biggest half marathon in terms of telecast, biggest athletes, prize money, etc. Today, the event is Delhi's calling card to the world.

CRICKET, TENNIS AND OTHER INDIAN SUCCESS STORIES

Why do some event managers and promoters mostly succeed, while others mostly don't? It is certainly not the quality of the idea alone. It involves conviction and a decision to see an idea through; it involves relationship management and an understanding of the country's current administrative policies, amongst other things. Here are some of the properties that proved to be a win as much for the brothers as for the cause of organised sports management in India.

The brothers unabashedly make the point that, 'Procam changed many dimensions of sport in India.' Well before distance running made Anil and Vivek Singh household names in sports, they had begun to revitalise, re-position and maybe even reconnect several sports in India. Tennis, for example, is watched and played widely in India today. The sport is organised and monetised. We have a good Davis Cup team and have had strong contenders in some Grand Slams as well. But, it was Anil and Vivek who first brought the French Open to Indian viewers via Doordarshan as early as 1996. Tennis was already there in the country by way of the National Series organised by the AITA (All India Tennis Association). However, the cumulative prize money was a modest INR 5,00,000 for the entire tournament, and players were expected to travel by train. They were expected to make their own arrangements to stay and ended up in hotels that were a far cry from today's standards or even international standards prevalent then. The brothers wanted to change all that. They wanted to arrange 5-star hotel stay and ground transport. They wanted to create a brand and re-position tennis and change the entire ecosystem. They realised their dream over the years with media events, promotional activities and after-parties around events. It brought the sport to the pages, the media started taking interest and suddenly families were willing to let their children take tennis seriously. For an entire decade (1989-98), the brothers organised the country's number one tennis tournament called the Indian Open. In all the years Procam ran the Indian Open, it went from being the Standard Chartered Indian Open to the Famous Grouse Indian Open and finally to the Gulf Oil Indian Open, in a clear indication that the tournament succeeded on the strength of the event rather than the might of the sponsor. They even did the ATP Challenger series and several smaller successful tennis event properties during that period.

'Procam changed many dimensions of sport in India.' Well before distance running made Anil and Vivek Singh household names in sports, they had begun to revitalise, re-position and maybe even reconnect several sports in India.

Procam's association with cricket has been similar. The largest school cricket programme in India and maybe even in Asia was the brainchild of Procam. Seventeen years ago, Procam decided to give youngsters in cricket professional exposure. In 1997, the Kellogs Cup was born for juniors between 14 and 16 years of age. It started across 100 schools in 2 cities. The objective was to make the youngster feel like a professional when he stepped onto the cricket field, and not like a kid. Branded gear, uniforms and cash awards (in place of biscuits that they got as prizes earlier!), were just some of the elements of the tournament that made it far more professional than anything the players had experienced before. They played at the Chinnaswami Stadium, the Police Grounds and other professional grounds. Today, the tournament has grown to cover 900 schools across 65 districts in India to become the largest inter-school cricket programme in the country. Cricketers like Ishant Sharma, Robin Uthappa and Gautam Gambhir have all been a part of this inter-school cricket programme that has proved to be one of the greatest feeders for the professional circuit.

Squash was another sport that the brothers pursued to put India on the global map. Today, we are winning gold medals in squash in international tournaments like the Commonwealth Games and we have some five or six players in the top 100 in the world. But it all started a long time ago. For six years, from 1993 to 1998, Anil and Vivek Singh managed the biggest squash tournament in the world in India. With the World Open in Qatar, they became the first company to do a world squash event trusted by a global body.

If we have come a long way in professional sports management in India, then we have even further to go and very many exciting plans on the anvil. Anil and Vivek Singh have plans to change yet another paradigm in sport. After capturing the country's imagination with distance running and other sports on land, the brothers now want to work their magic on water, or rather along the expansive coastline of Mumbai. The dream is to bring world-class power-boating to India. Not to an elite few, but to the entire community, to make it accessible and to make it broad enough to be a movement. Sadly, people stay away from beaches in India because nothing much has been done to keep them clean or develop them in any way. Procam wants to draw attention to this wonderful resource that we have and find engaging ways to interact with it. They want to bring infrastructure and life back into our coastlines. It is a tall order, but they have surmounted bigger challenges in the past to bring sport to the people. All we can do is wait with bated breath.

WHAT DOES IT TAKE TO DO SPORTS EVENTS AND SPORTS MANAGEMENT IN INDIA?

I could go on about several other wins, but at the core of this all is the attitude and wherewithal to make a success out of the industry in India. Sport is big in India, but the business of sport is set to get even bigger. Sport is driving social change, fostering peace and giving hope the world over. The potential to use sport to make a difference in India is immense: to create jobs, to develop opportunities and to put India on the global map. But big dreams can only be realised by taking small and measured steps to begin with.

What's in store for sports management in India is an array of new leagues across various sports, development and exponential growth of existing properties like the Mashal Sports promoted Pro-Kabaddi League and IMG Reliance promoted Indian Super League. In all this, the areas of sports sponsorships and marketing, sports statistics and analysis, sports celebrity management, sports IP creation, including design and conceptualisation are just some career opportunities to look forward to.

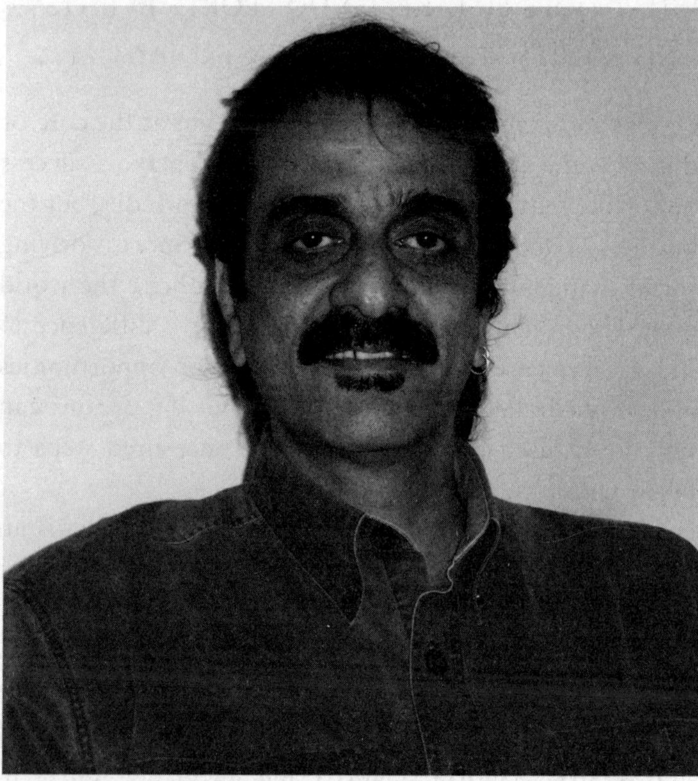

Brian Tellis, Chairman, Fountainhead Entertainment Pvt. Ltd.

3

BRANDS ON STAGE

With Brian Tellis, ***Fountainhead Entertainment Pvt. Ltd.***

A large part of the work day of an event manager goes by in managing events for brands. We also call these 'Corporate Events' or the 'Brand Activation Business'. They form a chunk of the revenues of most live event agencies. Several large and mid-size agencies depend primarily and sometimes entirely, on corporate business. Most often, brands commission agencies to conceptualise and manage events. Product / service / idea launches, stakeholder conferences, employee engagement events, incentive tours are typically events that fall in this genre.

Undoubtedly, there are many upsides to such commissioned corporate events. To begin with, they offer a chance to work with a variety of leading global brands and help shape some part of their story. Secondly, they are a godsend for the risk-averse. The industry norm is that brands pay an upfront advance of about 50 per cent as soon as the creative idea and execution plan are finalised. Agencies, in turn, have similar contracts with their suppliers and artists, so that they have to pay up only when they receive money themselves from the client (brand marketers).

Experiential agencies have thrived on this model well before the buzz around IP events became a drum roll! Both corporate commissioned events and Intellectual Property events have their own niches and cater to needs of consumers and marketers in very different ways. So, a happy co-existence for the two is the way of the future.

Brand marketers too have realised that events and activations offer a multi-sensory experience of the brand offering for the consumer like no other medium. At a time when consumers crave engagement every moment of their waking life, the opportunities for brands to engage them with relevant experiences are immense.

The question that faces us now is not whether the future of events is bright. That the Live Events industry is growing and will continue to do so exponentially is a foregone conclusion. The question is, that in an environment that is so conducive, how is it that only a handful of agencies have managed to break through the clutter?

A sure-shot way to stand out in the space of commissioned events is by upgrading skills and service levels to keep up with the times. Here is a look at how perspectives have changed in today's brand conversation universe. For example, it is not enough to be a compliant and amicable servicing person anymore. What an event manager of today needs to be, is someone who not only understands the brand, but is aware of the competitive scenario and can have a meaningful conversation with brand managers and even add to their knowledge base with inputs on experiential campaigns in that space. Again, it is not enough to have the latest technology that the industry has to offer; one must have an opinion on the best way to use the technology to make a connection with the consumer.

THE ENTERTAINMENT ECONOMY

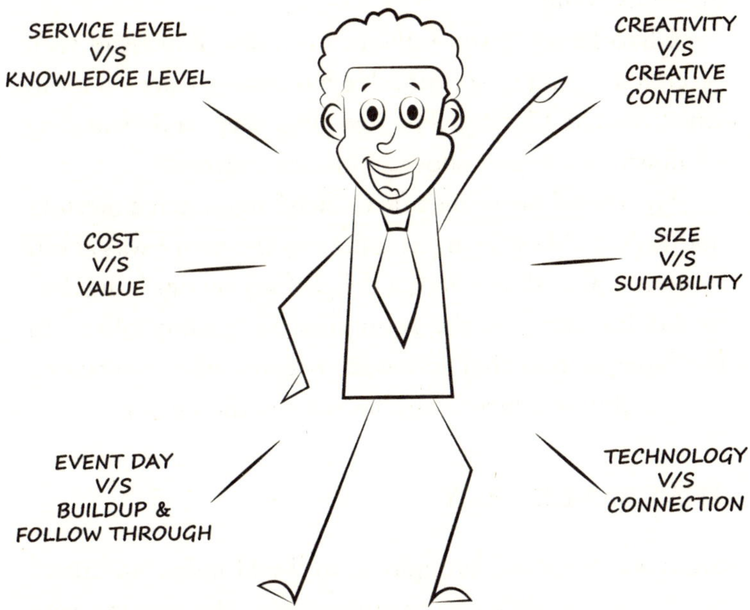

I caught up with Brian Tellis, who started off in events in his 20s, and has witnessed and championed several of these transitions in the evolution of the Live Events industry in India. Brian Tellis has been a man of the stage from the very beginning. He has three decades of expertise in the live entertainment business that spans creating and managing events, compering shows on stage and hosting radio shows (including the immensely popular show 'Tellis Like It Is'). He was a popular figure in the Bombay theatre circles in the 1990s. He is well respected as a storehouse of knowledge in events and has been on the jury of several prestigious entertainment industry award shows including the Channel [V] Awards, the MTV Video Music Awards and even the Holy Grail of them all — at Cannes.

I had heard Brian Tellis before I saw him. And then of course, I had to see him. He has been a voice on radio since August 15 1993. His love and deep understanding of music made him choose radio as a career.

He invited me to his office when I requested a meeting and I remember it being as quirky as the man I was about to meet. I was shown into a delightfully quaint bungalow in Bandra that was the Fountainhead flagship office. In the hour or two that followed, I learnt why events love Brian...and of course, why he returns the favour.

THAT BANDRA BOY

Brian was born and brought up in the Mumbai suburb of Bandra in a middle-income household. His parents were employed, though his mother gave up her job when the children were growing up because she wanted to spend more time with them. As parents, they encouraged both Brian and his elder sister to participate in extracurricular activities. Brian had always been very outgoing and a good sportsman, but too much of a free spirit to let textbooks pin him down. His penchant for skimming the surface of the hurdle with the same aplomb with which he made the pass percentage in exams, won him the nickname 'Hurdler' in school. Brian went to school in the 70s and 80s when scoring 80s and 90s in examinations clearly qualified one as a genius. Sixty was a really really good score. He explains, 'I wasn't less intelligent, but I was really bad if you looked at my report card. I was a sportsman, a hockey player. I was called a hurdler, because a hurdler's effectiveness besides speed was skimming the surface of the hurdle. The lower you are, the more effective. So if I needed 35 to pass, I had mastered the art of getting 36!'

Brian took to the world of engagement and entertainment very early in life. He got involved with the Bandra Zonals, an annual platform where the youngsters of the Catholic community battle it out over various performing arts. He says of the Zonals, 'I was a happy victim of that. It threw me into theatre; it threw me into singing and into a bit of social activity.' That early exposure to the community of talent and performers helped him set off on the path that would eventually become his calling.

'I was a happy victim of that (the Bandra Zonals event). It threw me into theatre; it threw me into singing and into a bit of social activity.' That early exposure to the community of talent and

performers helped him (Brian) set off on the path that would eventually become his calling.

HAPPY CAMPER

Brian has never been much of a conformist, but he grew up with the right values and knew his responsibilities well. 'I am a bit of a rock-and-roller. The sports, the music...I loved experimenting. I'm a maverick and a bit of a happy camper.' In all this, Brian never let his 9-to-5 down. He completed college and then pursued a diploma in Business Management. He went on to study Costing. Following in his father's footsteps, he started working with a pharmaceutical company in their finance department. Though Brian was good at numbers, his stint in pharma proved to be a bitter pill. He kept at it while also keeping his interests in theatre and music alive. A couple of jobs in finance departments were enough for Brian to realise that just being good at numbers cannot assure job satisfaction as a finance executive. So, since he loved travelling, he eventually moved to a sales and marketing job with Air Canada.

Brian's best decision at this time was to keep the other side of his life alive. He anchored shows, did theatre, sang jingles and kept up with music. And he did so in no small measure. He played a part in the legendary *Evita* with Alyque Padamsee and Sharon Prabhakar. He also did *Greased Lightening* with Shiamak Davar and Suneeta Rao. He was a part of a 4-member acoustic band called 'Voices' that played for 'Aid Bhopal' in 1985, which was the biggest concert the city had seen.

TODAY A TRAILBLAZER, BUT FOREVER A STUDENT

Brian never gave up on entertainment and entertaining people. As he puts it, 'It (the sphere of entertainment) was my passion and I am a student of entertainment. I loved doing it, I loved the lights and I make no excuses for it.' Brian told me about a pet indulgence that he admitted may sound childish. 'I still do what I did 30 years ago. I try to go to New York every couple of years. I spend one evening for sure, if not a couple more, sitting on Times Square and just soaking in the lights. I get laughed at, and patted on the back. I even get cups of tea from the neighbouring coffee shops. However this may sound, I love it.'

'It (the sphere of entertainment) has always been my passion and I am a student of entertainment. I loved doing it, I loved the lights and I make no excuses for it.'

Then, somewhere down the line, radio happened. On August 15, 1993, the day that private parties entered the radio business, Brian was on air. That is when Brian, along with partners Neale Murray and Otis D'Souza decided to start their own events agency, Fountainhead. In December 1993, when Brian decided to give up his steady job to start Fountainhead, his gut told him, as it always did, that he was going to make something of it. In fact, Brian had just had his second son when he decided to give up his job and start Fountainhead. The day he made his decision, he went back home and told his wife of 26 years (he had known her for 36!) about it. As it turned out, to Brian's surprise, she was as confident in his capability and decision-making ability as he was, and so Fountainhead was born without much heartbreak on the home front.

Fountainhead went on to become one of the best live event agencies in the commissioned events space, partly because Brian understood brands well. Today, Brian feels privileged that he is in a business that he loves. He started, like most agencies did, just going along with the client's brief. Only after more than a decade of growing organically, did he sit back and start to reflect on the DNA of his agency. Brian decided it was time to grow, not just organically, but exponentially. What set Brian and his agency apart in the Live Events industry is his philosophy and insight.

There are two ways in which brands and consumers engage in a live environment. One way is the brand-first approach where the nucleus of the idea emanates from the brand. Commissioned events usually have this approach. The brand has a fairly clear idea about what it wants to do. Agencies add value and ideas to create an event for consumers that communicate the brand's objectives. The other approach is consumer-first, where the nucleus of the idea emanates from a consumer need. This is the approach IP events have. While creating an IP, an agency starts with the consumer and works to create content that people want to spend time with. Brands that fit that idea are then integrated into the property as sponsors and partners. Brian started with and has made his mark through commissioned events, but is steadily working towards capturing more of the entertainment ecosystem. He says, 'Over a period of time we inflected, and we realised pretty early that clients wanted more. They said that since we were doing their events, we should really expand the scope to what precedes and follows it. I have always believed that if you're doing an event, there needs to be a build-up and follow-through. For instance, if we are spending INR 100 on an event, it is often prudent to spend 50% as a build up to it and perhaps 25% post the event to maximise the effectiveness of the show. Mind you, this can't be a generalisation, but is a possibility with a large number of events.' In a chat with him, he tells me about his endeavour to cover both the above approaches of 'brand-first' and 'consumer-first', and everything in between.

Fountainhead, being a classic case, started off with what was traditionally known as commissioned events. Along with trying to grow business and a client base, Brian backward integrated into a specific offering within events to start a separate production division called Production Terminus with a separate P&L from the mainstream agency. Soon, while continuing to look at the brand and client, Brian also started focusing on the consumer and the market. It is then that he started an IP offering under the brand name Oranjuice Entertainment.

IP was a learning curve and a very exciting one at that. 'We started, through their eyes, to look at the consumer and work upwards (or backwards) to the brand. Understand consumer behaviour, understand consumer needs, and see what their preferred mediums of communication were depending on the target audience.' Brian has always felt that IP is about starting with the consumer and their needs, to create content that they want, and then connecting with a brand that would be ideal to bring it to them. From an ideation and planning point of view, this was pretty much the opposite of commissioned events, where we get a brief from brands, understand the brand, and then work towards creating an event that would engage the consumer. With IPs, the focus shifts from the brands-first approach, to the consumer-first approach.

AN IDEA IS AS GOOD AS ITS EFFECTIVENESS

Brian found that along the way, brands started asking how we can maximise effectiveness and engage with the consumer more closely. That is when he decided to extend his involvement in consumer experiences and start a division to handle MICE (Meetings, Incentive tours, Conferences and Exhibitions). This hit the ground running.

One thing was clear from my interaction with Brian. There is a great deal to be learnt from him in terms of creating depth in service offerings. Several agencies specialise in certain aspects of events while being competent to handle other industry-related verticals too. For instance, an agency's mainstay may be corporate events, but it could do some wedding business or ground promotions as well. Brian and his team had mastered the art of creating a near-complete offering for a brand. Brian is a firm believer of maximising effectiveness. He feels that we really cannot focus all our energies on creating and delivering the 'event-day' experience. There is a build-up around most events, and a follow-through. We must focus our energies on completing the loop. Brian highlights, 'The client is now not just looking for you to own the logistics and the management of the logistics, but they are looking for you to own the larger idea (IP). Now they are looking for you to own the audience around it as well.' Fountainhead Digital was born when he realised that an event could only reach out to a finite number of people. While it is true that events cover the last crucial mile in consumer engagement, their impact is deep rather than wide. Clients are now looking for agencies to own more of the ecosystem.

REACHING OUT WIDE, BUT NEVER LOSING TOUCH WITH THE DEPTH

Brian explains how dealing with brands keeps him on his toes, and how brands themselves must stay agile as well. He says, 'To me, the vision is growing brands through experiences. Everything from the Last Supper to you and me sitting across the table today is an experience. How then do brands navigate the journey to tell a consistent story? In any journey, there are stages — when the right discipline is required, food for growth is required, the right parentage or values are required, shaping thoughts, mannerisms and grooming are all required. Once a brand personality is developed, then it's time to go out there and make the most of it, monetize it. Eventually every brand reaches a stage where it needs to give back to society after all that it has received. There are innumerable experiences and messages in this constant cycle, and we are there to deliver it when the time is right.'

So, experiences differ along the path of the brand life cycle, but what does it really mean when we say we want to own more of the experiential ecosystem? 'To me, the vision is growing brands through experiences. Our excitement comes from journeying with a brand,' explains Brian. The life of a brand is an experiential journey. There is not a single brand that can afford to go by its entire life cycle with just a single kind of event or promotion. Like he explained before, the brand journey can be likened to the journey of life, where we need a different kind of atmosphere and experiences as children (discipline, right food, values) and quite another set as adults (focus shifts to application of values and skills acquired) etc., and towards the end of the cycle, it is time to give back. Brands, similarly, have different stages of their life cycle that call for very different solutions and experiences for the brand itself and the consumer. Brands need to re-invent themselves along the way because competition and circumstances make change necessary and beneficial. You might chart a course, but you must also have an ear to the ground and be ready to adapt when the time is right along the way. 'If your alignment is to a brand and its growth, or to consumers and their ever-evolving needs, then you must be in a position to understand behavioural patterns of both brand and consumer, and if possible, offer solutions for whichever phase of the journey they are in.' In the live events space Brian has redefined this journey in the verticals that he has expanded into. This, to him, is a way of influencing more of the ecosystem than he can if he is involved with just the core of corporate or brand events.

'To me, the vision is growing brands through experiences. Our excitement comes from journeying with a brand.'

Let us take an example. Let us say that Brian and his team have been doing branded events for a particular client for years. They now say that they have reached the pinnacle and want to do something in the live events space that becomes a legacy, and which their brand will be known for, for a swatch of time, then it helps that the agency is in a position where it can suggest, plan and create an event property (IP). Or if the brand feels they want to attach a heart to their initiatives, they want to do CSR, or they want to speak to every school going child in the country, then what is needed is a national school contact programme, which is a series of mini events and engagement activities conducted within schools with the help of the school administration, and brought to the children by the brand. They may all be within the experiential space, but they certainly are different animals that need very different thought processes and skill sets. It is for that very reason that Brian runs each of these divisions as separate operation units that function independently while feeding off each other intellectually.

But is it enough to spread yourself to cover a wider gamut? To have a core offering and to build around it is certainly an advantage, but Brian is very clear about what sets him and his team apart. 'We have chosen to be a hard-core research and thinking agency and offer a few services along with it. But we are clear about one thing. While the larger part of our business is the roll-out or the operations, the focus area for us is really the ideation, the design and the planning. We, as an agency, are clear about that. That is what we believe creates long-term relationships (with a brand and their consumers).' He goes on to say that this industry does not have much of an entry barrier. Practically, anyone with a phone, a laptop and a desk can choose to be an event manager. A strong differentiator is key to success. Brian insists money motivates him, but not as much as the desire to be known as an agency with a soul. 'That is what we try and do in every event and with every brand. On occasion, a brand might choose not to go with us for some reason or another. But we would like to leave behind a little calling card that says "Those guys were special".' The brand speak would be, 'I enjoyed that flirtation because they had a bit of heart or soul in their thought.' If you look at any of the events that have come off Brian's drawing board, like the Celebrate Bandra event or Mahindra Blues, they all have a heart, a softer aspect.

'We have chosen to be a hard-core research and thinking agency and offer a few services along with it. But we are clear about one thing. While

the larger part of our business is the roll-out or the operations, the focus area for us is really the ideation, the design and the planning. We as an agency, are clear about that.'

They say success never comes easy. Brian has always followed his heart, walked the path less trodden and never regretted it. But there came a time four-odd years ago when he came face-to- face with the inevitable 'life-lesson'. Brian and team decided to create some verticals in the pursuit of expanding service offerings in the live domain. Up until then, they had grown organically and cautiously, expanding as the need arose or when prodded by the client. They decided at one point, to put themselves out there and grow exponentially. Brian never had investors, so they invested in growing verticals and in a short time found themselves cash-strapped. They came out of it alright, but it taught Brian an important lesson. Plan for growth or be ready to grow again!

STAYING GROUNDED

Brian has clearly seen far more successes than disappointments in his career, and under these circumstances, it is hard to remain grounded. So I asked what keeps him grounded and he related a delightful story.

In 1996, Brian and his wife were invited, as a part of a Citibank Visa promotion, to see the London Olympics. Brian's agency, Fountainhead, was in its honeymoon phase, and everything was going right. Brian was brimming with the confidence that comes from knowing that he had a good start and was good at his work. Perfect timing to be brought back down to Earth! In his words, 'I was AMAZED to experience it (the Olympics) first hand. You talk about organisation, about thousands of athletes coming together...you want logistics? Try this!' Brian saw it all happen seamlessly in front of him. He sat there, just soaking in the excitement — from the lighting of the Olympic torch by Muhammad Ali, to seeing the greatest athletes of the world on the field; from watching Andre Agassi to Michael Jordan. He saw Leander win his Olympic Bronze. The experience was beyond anything money could buy. Needless to say, it turned out to be an event that left a lasting impression on Brian. It was extremely humbling for him to understand the kind of planning it must take to manage an event that is truly global — an experience way beyond logistics. Brian puts it very simply, 'Every time I get too big for my own head, I think of things like this and tell myself to relax and get down to work!'

IT IS NOW OR NEVER FOR LIVE EVENTS

By the time you read this, the new government will be over two years old. Even now, as from the very beginning, the political atmosphere does seem conducive to the growth of live events. Consumers, India Inc. and everyone in between (meaning us agency types), have come out emphatically in favour of the new wave of change. Brian pointed out a few things that augur very well for the Live

Events industry. The first is that there will be a stable economic sentiment, and that controls a large part of the purse strings. The second very good thing is that there was style and panache in how the election campaign was done. It was high on experience. Mr Narendra Modi used holograms in villages! A hologram projection is a life-sized, three-dimensional projection of an image which makes it seem almost real. The BJP had thousands of rallies where Mr Modi (as a hologram) spoke to people. There were people who actually believed the hologram to be the man himself and requested to meet him! Such was the impact and integration of experiential marketing.

Even more heartening is the 'Make in India' initiative. As international brands look afresh at the Indian market and the possibility of doing business here, experiential agencies will need to establish the connection between these brands and our communities. Simultaneously, administrations across the country are gearing up to facilitate the creation of smart cities. Connected consumers mean more access to entertainment and even higher involvement of indigenous as well as international brands in bringing entertainment to people across the country.

The expected general sentiment will be to encourage on-ground experiences and events. And since we are a nation that loves getting together, interacting and celebrating, things are likely to speed up for us.

Devraj Sanyal, Managing Director and CEO, Universal Music Group & EMI Music, South Asia

4

HITTING THE RIGHT NOTES

*With Devraj Sanyal, **Universal Music Group & EMI Music***

Music is to entertainment what entertainment is to us. If entertainment is our release, then music is entertainment's lease of life. In fact, apart from reading, I can't think of too many other forms of entertainment that don't involve music. Right from concerts, down to music interludes between stand-up comedy acts, music has the wherewithal to win consumers or wean them away from a piece of engagement.

As with every other industry on the planet, the digital wave has swept across music. According to the FICCI-KPMG Indian Media and Entertainment Industry Report 2014, digital (music) revenues which contributed 53% of the industry, are expected to contribute about 62% by 2018. Technology has truly changed the way music is produced, distributed and consumed. It has facilitated access to music on the go in a way that is far more exciting than carrying around a bank of 200 songs. Streaming has made it possible to access a million songs from wherever you are, whenever you want it. What makes this particularly impactful is its mass appeal and accessibility. It is not just a select few who have this benefit. With the proliferation of budget smartphones and reasonable data plans, consumers across the country have integrated music with every waking moment of their lives.

One would expect this ubiquitous accessibility of music to reduce the popularity of live music events. After all, if you have constant access to music from across the world, wouldn't you be less inclined to seek out music events? Is a 'live' experience worth buying tickets, going out of home, finding parking (or means of transport) and spending some serious money? Apparently it is. Figures show[1] that while the overall growth in the music industry fell for the first time in years in 2013, 'Public Performance' bucked the trend by growing 20% in 2013, over 2012. Music IPs and festivals across the globe are growing in popularity. Live music properties like Sunburn, held annually in Goa see tens of thousands of youngsters book tickets months in advance and plan for this annual trip for about a year. The Mahindra Blues Festival, while being niche, has its set of die-hard fans. Bigger, global examples include the electronic music festival Tomorrowland in Belgium and Sensation which has a global footprint. While live performances are evergreen and growth-drivers of music consumption, they are just a part of the consumption mix.

---

1 Overall size and growth projections by KPMG in India analysis and industry estimates, as quoted in the FICCI-KPMG Indian Media and Entertainment Industry Report 2014.

MODES OF CONSUMPTION

I had requested to meet Devraj Sanyal to throw light on the evolution of music in the live events arena because he is known in the industry as *the* professional who can speak authoritatively on the creative aspect of music as well as the business of music. I was a little intimidated as I walked into his office, not only because his cabin at the Universal Music office is bigger than some entire agency offices, but also because I saw a large framed picture of

Gurmeet Ram Rahim Singh or Guruji, of MSG fame (Yes, I am going to explain this later in the chapter). I'm not sure if I was shocked or awestruck, but I fumbled my way to a large and stylishly black leather chair and was immediately put at ease by the easy-going Devraj Sanyal.

A musician himself, Devraj Sanyal has been a part of India's vastly popular heavy metal band Brahma since 1994. In his current leadership role with Universal, he is charged with the management and operational running of all Universal Music Group businesses in the region.

MUSIC DISCOVERS DEVRAJ

Devraj discovered his musical side in his college years, but as it turned out later, it was he who was quite a find for the Indian music industry because he went on to pioneer initiatives that shaped the way music was made available in India. Let's start at the beginning. Devraj was born in Kolkata (then Calcutta), but brought up in Mumbai. He didn't have any roots in music, but sometime in college, he got together with some friends and formed a band called Brahma. It's been 21 years, and the band members still find time between their day jobs to play together. Because he has always been in touch with music and been a musician longer than he has been in the business side of the industry, Devraj is confident that he can be as creatively discerning as clinically profitable. He declares, 'Nowhere in the world is there a musician-MD; I want to be the first.' Devraj adds that he has an edge because he has been a musician for years. He says, 'When you are trying to run a business, but you are just a suit who doesn't understand music at a fundamental level, then you are simply in a trading business.'

Devraj started his career between 1990 and 1995. He started off on his own in events at a time when the industry was at its infancy, with only a handful of players. After a few years, he moved on to a job in ad sales for *Elle* magazine. He then spent 15 years in events before joining his current role as the head of Universal Music in India. Besides his entrepreneurial work in events, he also set up *Times of India*'s events division called 360 degrees in 1999, and between 2000 and 2010, Devraj was the CEO of Percept and headed all their verticals apart from advertising and media.

LIVE IS EVERGREEN

Devraj says that as early as in the 90s, it became apparent that entertainment was going to grow, it was going to explode over the next few decades. However, problems were expected to temper exponential growth. 'We always knew that we were fundamentally a piracy-driven market where it was cool to have everything for free. But somehow, the only thing we ever paid for was (live) entertainment,' says Devraj. Some agencies recognised this years ago and created IPs like IIFA, Sunburn, etc. Devraj was a co-creator of the hugely successful electronic music festival Sunburn that is still probably India's biggest IP event on ground. About Sunburn and its almost inexplicable popularity he says, 'Will somebody pay INR 120 to buy a Tiesto album?

No. Will somebody pay INR 4000 to go and see him live? Oh yes.' Sunburn, which was in its 9th year when I met Devraj is a testament to this insight.

This behavioural pattern of seeking experiences is primarily social, feels Devraj. 'The new generation clearly has an affinity to experience rather than consume content.' By the 4th year of the Sunburn Festival they already had a capacity size of about 40,000 to 45,000 people. This, despite the fact that the festival was held in Goa, which is expensive to get to, and at a time of the year (December) when peak-season rates apply to both, travel and accommodation. The young generation keeps swarming to festivals like these because of the immense peer-approval that accompanies attendance. It is very 'cool' to be seen in one of these festivals, and makes for some dream profile pictures! Only a handful started attending IP events and festivals a decade ago, but live acts are now practically mainstream entertainment, with tickets available at about the same price as a top end film ticket.

'The new generation clearly has an affinity to experience rather than consume content.'

The live music festival is a completely different animal. The music that the average Indian consumes in his personal space may well be very different from the genre he chooses to consume live. The Mahindra Blues Festival has its steady set of followers who could live without a whole lot of blues music for the rest of the year. Similarly, the young fans of the Sunburn Festival may mostly choose to listen to Bollywood music or rock in their personal time, but spend the few days of the Sunburn Festival living on EDM (Electronic Dance Music).

LIVE IS, AND WILL CONTINUE TO BE, THE BIG DADDY OF MUSIC

Devraj divides the entire legal music consumption business in three buckets. The first is **consumed music.** This includes download subscriptions, purchase of music CDs and the like, but the download ecosystem is dying according to Devraj. It is streaming, popularised by companies like Spotify, Pandora, Gaana, Hungama, Saavn or Wynk, that's the future. Physical consumption of music through downloads and CDs are fast making way for technology-powered consumption led by streaming. The real problem that plagues this aspect of the music business is 'Freemiumisation', or the tendency of rights owners to give away too much for free in an attempt to win over a larger consumer base. Simply put, free music subscriptions give consumers access to so much music so conveniently, that consumers rarely feel the need to upgrade to premium 'paid' subscriptions even if it comes at a small cost. Often the only price a consumer has to pay to access free music legally is an advertisement break once in every couple of songs.

The second and biggest bucket is **experiential.** According to Devraj, not only does the live music space drive the music business, it also drives live events in general. As far as live entertainment on ground goes, music and comedy lead the charge and virtually make up the entire pie. He estimates that the ratio between the two is 80:20 or even 90:10 in favour of music. There are a lot of IP events around Bollywood, but these are more for television consumption than for ground. This huge chunk of business, called the live music industry segment is layered. Companies in the music business can operate as booking agents or music promoters, or both. Devraj and the team at Universal Music and EMI operate mainly as booking agents, with concrete plans to venture more deeply into the IP or music promotion space in the near future. At the grassroot level, as booking agents, they work with artists of varying genres, calibre and experience to send them for live music tours globally, sponsored shows for clients or even special performances at social events like weddings. At the higher end of the scale is the music IP business, or Intellectual Property events; where a lot of effort and resources are put into making it a brand. Devraj cites the example of 'Live Love Laugh Shaan Se'. 'A Shaan doing Live Love Laugh, is a musical IP, where he is singing Kishore, Rafi and RD Burman songs in a fully scripted show. So Indie artists, who are also Bollywood-facing, singing old Bollywood songs in a massive choreographed effort, is a big draw. Consumers could go to the NCPA (National Centre for the Performing Arts) and buy a ticket to watch the unique show.' At the top of the rung is the live music festival space. That is where festivals like Sunburn and Independence Rock feature. According to Devraj Sanyal all these rungs hold immense potential and will drive the live music business in the coming decade. While stand-alone music tours and performances at social events are low-hanging fruit and potential cash cows, the sustainable format that will benefit the industry in the long run, is music festivals and IPs. If sustained patiently, developed and built over years, festivals can become highly profitable ventures, with lasting brand value and recall amongst consumers.

The third bucket, and a very important one because of the potential for music owners to monetise, is **branded music content**. Currently small, but very fast growing, branded content is the new kid on the block. Devraj says, 'Brands are a ***huge*** part of our ecosystem. I don't think enough people give this aspect due credit, and we (Universal Music and EMI) are forerunners in it.' By way of an example, he cites HP Connected Music (HP: Hewlett Packard Enterprise). This is a technology developed by Universal Music for HP, where HP customers can have access to approximately one and a half million songs for free through a tile on the Windows 8 platform on their HP device. Customers can access, stream, port and download all the music they want for free, without paying Universal Music anything. It is HP who has paid the music label to bring this offering as a value-add to their customers. It is a co-developed property, but one that is owned by the music company so that they can sell it to another brand at a future date. Co-developing with brands is very high on Devraj's agenda as it is a fast-growing and extremely profitable aspect of the music business. A live music example of co-developing with brands is the #GioneeTROT, an electronic music festival on the trot, co-developed by Universal Music and Gionee. It helps smartphone-maker Gionee bring the increasingly popular EDM music genre to their customers across the country. The winning aspect of these events is that it gives music fans in several cities access to live, technologically sophisticated EDM music concerts, that they would have otherwise had to travel to a Goa or a Delhi to experience. The Indore leg had 800 people buying tickets for a venue that had a capacity of 700, because this was a chance to experience an EDM festival for INR 1000-1500 in one's own backyard. As Devraj puts it, 'It's a good-looking event. It looks like a Sunburn or a Supersonic poster, and the young kids end up saying, "I don't have to go someplace else, it's coming to me, and it's mine".'

'Brands are a huge part of our ecosystem. I don't think enough people give this aspect due credit, and we (Universal Music and EMI) are forerunners in it.'

Though all three buckets of consumed music, live music and branded content are distinct, there are areas of overlap. For example, Shraddha Sharma is an artist who may perform at a live event. The minute a brand is paying for her to play, it falls between being an experiential live event and branded content. All in all, every one of these buckets has the potential to drive music consumption and business for labels in the future.

THE FUTURE OF MUSIC

Globalisation, increased connectivity and access to Internet on the go, have increased the array of choices for the consumer. Entertainment businesses are, therefore, struggling to remain relevant and profitable in this scenario. The question of what the future holds and how best entertainment companies can ride the wave of consumption is more relevant now than ever before.

Devraj explains, 'My business is not just a label business, not at all!' His vision for the structure of the music business for his company, from 2013 to 2016 includes live events as a significant and central element that is expected to drive business. He says that on an average he does 20 to 30 live musical events a month of varying size and scale. The business covers music talent management, has its own publishing assets, runs a full-service 'music ad-agency', includes music merchandising and every aspect that is required to find talent, create music from scratch and deliver it. An aspect of his business that is slowly growing and contributing handsomely to figures is content for clients. I had begun this chapter saying that Devraj's office has a framed picture of Gurmeet Ram Rahim Singh, the highly controversial saint or Guruji. Devraj's team handled all his music and went on to sell 10 million copies! Yes, that many. That's as many copies as an international artist like Adele would sell. No one in the Indian music fraternity has got to this number in the recent past. Clearly, content produced solely for a client makes tremendous sense and Devraj and the team have spotted this early on. He says music content creation is very different from music you would create for a brand if you are an advertising agency because in that case, all you need to do is create a jingle and hand it over to the brand. In case of the content business, the entire sales cycle is addressed. In Devraj's words, 'We become the arm to distribute, produce, create / co-create as well as handle social media content around it if needed. It starts with recording and producing, and goes on to selling to the brands' followers and collecting.' The beauty of this segment is that it uses all parts of Universal Music's value system, ensuring that the business prospects are optimised. Says Devraj, 'We do this because it uses all parts of our ecosystem. Every business we do must use as many value ports as possible from within the system.'

DEVRAJ SANYAL ON TRENDS OF THE MUSIC INDUSTRY

Live music is about the fastest-growing segment and will be a major growth area to look out for in the years to come, according to Devraj Sanyal. As the co-founder of Sunburn which was the trailblazer of live music festivals in India, Devraj understands the live space and his instincts about the business have proved right time and again. Live Events is a business that is growing at double digits every year — Devraj estimates it to be in the region of 30%. He says, 'The IP business in the next five years will be as big as my overall business today.'

'The IP business in the next five years will be as big as my overall business today.'

Digital-savvy and technology-fronted business model: With India set to have over 650[2] million smartphones over the next three years, newer offerings that use the digital route are bound to hit the ground running. The HP Connected Music example mentioned earlier is one such endeavour.

Streaming is undoubtedly the future of personal music consumption. The 'on-demand' model has long replaced the traditional model of fixed schedules. Prices are ridiculously low. As Devraj put it, 'If all it takes is INR 100 to get all the legitimate music on the planet, then why not?' When 4G technology comes into effect through telecom infrastructure, streaming will only become more of an attraction. Moreover, credit cards and payment gateways are getting more popular and becoming increasingly secure. All this is facilitating the proliferation of streaming. The download economy is dead. All people download these days is a caller tune. The rest is all streaming.

Devraj has always believed in adopting the **Blue Ocean** strategy. He has always chosen to steer clear of the crowded Bollywood music space despite having the resources and muscle power to handle it. Rather, he has chosen to pursue and make a business of new and unexplored genres like branded content, tech platforms and merchandising. Devraj opines, 'To me, if I'm in a business that cannot actually effect change, then I'd rather not be in it. I'd rather hang my boots.'

---

2 Study by networking solutions major Cisco, as published in the *Economic Times* on Feb 13, 2015

'To me, if I'm in a business that cannot actually effect change, then I'd rather not be in it. I'd rather hang my boots.'

Another effort in this direction is video. Devraj says, **'Video is the new audio.'** This is the age of the 'YouTube stars' who can now have fan followings larger than some Bollywood stars. Multi-channel is something Devraj and the team at Universal Music are now exploring seriously, with an aim to delivering quality video content in the near future.

F&B bundled with entertainment is a great business model for live music. Blue Frog and Bonobo are successful examples.

POPULISM VERSUS INDUSTRY WELFARE — WHERE SHOULD THE INDUSTRY DRAW THE LINE?

Whether in politics or business, populism is a sensitive issue. The music industry has perhaps gone a little too far in pandering to the masses. 'Freemium', or the amount of freebies that the music industry offers, can become counter-productive to the industry, according to Devraj Sanyal. Music streaming websites have a user base of anything between 50 to 70 million customers, but the truth is that only a miniscule proportion are actually paid subscribers. Though free, these are legal sources of accessing music. The larger issue is piracy and Devraj believes that the industry still has a long way to go and needs to up the efforts to curb this menace. He feels there are two things that need to be done. First, the industry will make it increasingly easier to consume music, and secondly, it shall make it really tough to do so for free. One way to do this is to make free music very annoying with a series of interruptions.

The industry is also pursuing the matter through the law. Says Devraj, 'In 2012, we won a historic judgement where we got 382 sites shut down because they were serving pirated music.' The Supreme Court ruled in the industry's favour and this resulted in various Internet service providers denying access to the banned sites. This was a historic victory and a big step towards a 'Swachh' consumption economy. The ideal goal is to be in a situation where consumers will have no option but to legitimately consume music, and it won't be cool to get music for free anymore because of the stigma attached to piracy.

WHAT NEXT FOR DEVRAJ...

The voice behind Brahma is now the face behind 'The Stage'. As one of the judges (along with Vishal Dadlani, Ehsaan Noorani and Monica Dogra) of the first English music talent hunt on Colours Infinity, Devraj is now exploring yet another facet of the music business. He believes that 'It's about the art of business, not about the art of trade. In my opinion, the ones who ultimately count in the world are the ones who actually created breakthrough business ahead of their time.' Devraj wants to write a book and open a music school sometime in the future. Considering the wealth of knowledge and experience he possesses, copies of the book, like his music records, are likely to fly off the shelves (or maybe digital shelves, knowing his penchant for tech!).

'It's about the art of business, not about the art of trade. In my opinion, the ones who ultimately count in the world are the ones who actually created breakthrough business ahead of their time.'

Martin da Costa, Chief Executive Officer, Seventy Event Media Group

5

OF WEDDINGS, FESTIVALS AND ENGLISH SENSIBILITIES

With Martin da Costa, ***Seventy Event Media Group***

The access to knowledge and information is now 'virtually' unlimited. This ensures that Indians have a wealth of options to choose from while making any decision. This is true even as far as entertainment is concerned. From eating out and shopping, to watching world cinema or maybe learning a foreign language; anything can capture India's imagination and add to the wealth of 'experience'.

The Live Events industry has always been a breeding ground for new and exciting ideas and entertainment options. I would go as far as to say that the industry thrives on novelty and change. It often happens that a brand manager of a multi-national corporation sees an entertainment act, or an event setup structure, or maybe even a new variety of lights (if he is particularly observant). He then comes back to India and requests his live events agency to contract the same for shows in India for his brand. Agencies are only too happy to comply as long as money matters are taken care of. Not only does it add to the reputation of an agency as a first mover in adopting something new and exciting, it also becomes an idea that can be applied to other briefs and events depending on suitability. Even more often, proprietors and directors of large event companies travel abroad and attend trade fairs specifically to scout for such innovations. This trend can work the other way around as well. India offers a wealth of culture, entertainment and other live experiences. Traditional dance and martial arts forms, yoga and regional arts are just some of India's exports to the world.

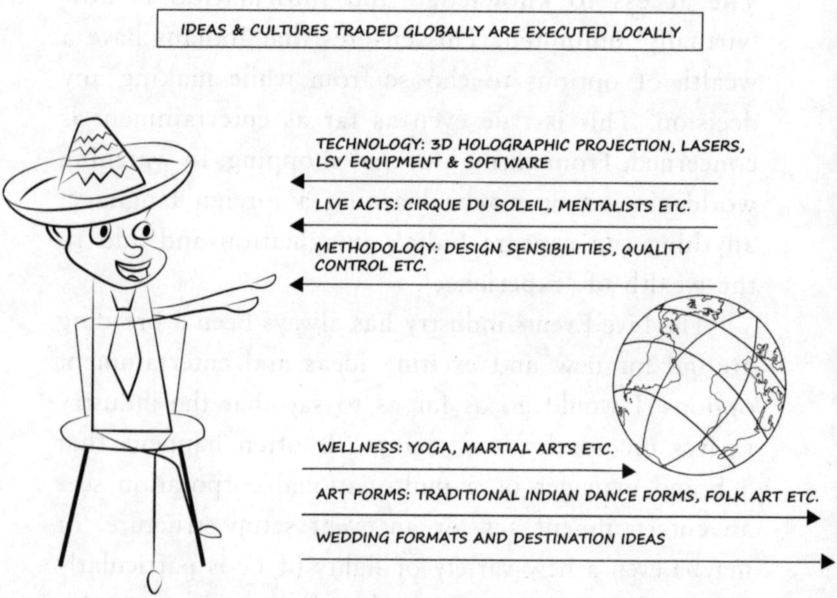

While writing this book and doing my research, I discovered that our Live Events industry absolutely craves new ideas and influences. This is a client-driven phenomenon. So, while the post-recession trend shows clients holding back on event spends and squeezing agency profit margins, novelty is one factor that completely bucks this trend! The prospect of a technology, act or experience that has never been done in India, or at least, never been done in a certain way, is indeed priceless in the minds of clients. Half-British, half-Portuguese events icon Martin da Costa identified this key route to chart a successful career in the Live Events industry in India.

As the CEO of Seventy Event Media Group, Martin da Costa arrived in India in 1995 to set up an indigenous company based on all his international experiences. Today, the company is regarded as one of the pioneers of luxury events and destination management in India.

LONDON TO MUMBAI

Martin was born in Portugal and went to boarding school in London. He went on to study at the London School of Economics, and while most of his classmates pursued Banking or Law, Martin chose to go down the road less travelled. He did start off doing stints with Unilever and Procter & Gamble, but the whole thing looked really boring, so he decided to follow his heart and practically hustled a job in sports marketing in the recessionary market of the early 90s in England. 'Entertainment, sport and art is a brilliant environment to be in,' says Martin, clearly still very enamoured by the industry that he has helped shape in India.

Martin was working with a large sports marketing agency in London called Parallel Media Group, primarily doing massive golf and tennis events across the world. At the age of 24, he was Head of Marketing there and came down to India because the agency wanted to set up Parallel Media here. He was here for 2-3 months when he met Mr Amitabh Bachchan and his brother Ajitabh. The conversation went so well that within 5 days, ABCL made Martin an offer, gave him a signing bonus, found him an apartment and put him in India to set up a sports marketing agency. However, in 1995-96, cricket was the only sport that had national viewership, so Martin moved on to another aspect of live entertainment. By then, he had completely fallen in love with India and had decided to stay here. He went on to fall in love with an Indian singer and artist who he pursued and eventually won over. Martin and Sagarika got married on the beaches of Kashid in the true style of a couple wedded to entertainment.

OLD HABITS DIE HARD

Martin started handling Indipop artists in 1997 because Indipop looked like it could make a dent in the Bollywood film music market. There was Lucky Ali, Shaan and Sagarika, Raageshwari, etc., who had become really popular. However, Martin, who was still learning the ropes in a new country with a completely new culture, figured soon enough that Indipop, though popular would eventually get subsumed by Bollywood. In any case, by 1997-98, Martin and the team created an event property called The

Peace Concert, at a time when India and Pakistan were at loggerheads over their nuclear capabilities. The concert was created as an effort at peace and to draw attention to the problems between the two countries. It was, in a sense, one of the first music 'festivals' in India, because it went on for 9 straight hours with 50 artists getting on stage. It happened in Mumbai at the Andheri Sports Complex with an audience of 20,000-30,000 youngsters. It was this concert that took Martin down the concert and event management route in India. It was because of this concert that he started reaching out to the big brands in India like Coca Cola and ITC.

It was at this time that Martin made one of the most important decisions of his career, and one that set the tone for a niche that he eventually carved for himself in the live entertainment industry of India. Martin and his team at Seventy EMG started working with brands on their events. In 2000-2001, when brands started requiring and asking for activation and brand promotion services, Martin realised that it was something that he was not comfortable venturing into. He saw large FMCGs hiring 2000-odd youth from slums to stand on streets with banners. Martin decided then that he wanted nothing to do with this business. Brand activations and promotions were not for him. I believe this might have had something to do with his upbringing. He was new to the country where managing unorganised manpower in large numbers was a daunting task. To him, with his Western sensibilities, it just seemed out of control. Undoubtedly, quality control in large-scale street promotions is next to impossible, but large Indian agencies had managed to create a format with checks at every level to make the process as smooth as possible. Yet, there were bound to be glitches, something Martin consciously decided to steer clear of. In Martin's words, 'I could see that the margins of that business were getting tighter and tighter by the day and that there was little or no room for creativity. It was about bringing the brand to people as cheaply as possible and I did not see how I or Seventy EMG could add any value.' He chose careful planning / execution in controlled environments over exponential growth and numbers. This defined him in the years to come.

'I could see that the margins of that business (brand promotions) were getting tighter and tighter by the day and that there was little or no room for creativity. It was about bringing the brand to people as cheaply as possible and I did not see how I or Seventy EMG could add any value.'

IDENTIFYING A NICHE

A lot of talented people set out to make a career in events in India in the 90s, but only a handful ended up on top of the game. Each of them has a story to tell, of how they identified their strengths and added value to clients in a way that only they could. For some, it is a story of size and scale. Some others win with creativity and content. Martin believes he made a difference by being a stickler for quality execution and design of international standards for clients in the luxury and lifestyle segment. This he did even if it was at the cost of scale. So while other larger agencies had 150-180 employees, between 1997 and 2005, Martin's team had less than 25 people. However, he estimates that Seventy EMG would have been making the same amount of money as their larger counterparts who he believes must have had profitability issues because of the sheer size of the offices.

When asked about how he decided on this unusual positioning for his agency, he proudly says that he and his team have an excellent track record as far as event execution goes. The only times they have ever had a problem in execution quality is when they have bowed to budget pressures from the client, for instance, the time when they took on a temple launch and were under tremendous budgetary pressures. They were handling more than 5 million people over 4 days. There were more than 2 million people per day to be fed. Martin had to hire over 2,500 waiters for a miniscule budget and ended up getting people off the streets even though it was against their better judgement. It ended in a fiasco and the client was very upset. Martin realised that he had put in 3 months of planning and execution in an event that ultimately left everyone fuming. That was when he realised that he just should have put his foot down. He vowed to never compromise on money again if he could help it. Martin, who comes from a very different background, observes, 'In India, money is such an emotional thing. People are so wrapped up about saving money that they often lose sight of the big picture. It does not happen anywhere else I have worked.' That is how Martin learned pretty early on in his career to just say 'No'.

Consequently, the events that Martin did were always 'fairly high-end'. He believes, 'There weren't many luxury brands in India at that time, but for example, we would get a brand manager from ITC who would want an event done in a certain way. There would be no other agency he would go to. He would come to us, and we would design and run it, so that it looked somewhat international.' Maybe this was possible because he did not have other distractions like pitching for activation businesses that kept some of his competitors busy.

In a bid to keep his profitability healthy, Martin always charged a premium fee for event services. He explains, 'We used to turn down more briefs than we would take if we sensed that the brand didn't have the money or couldn't afford us. We were always more expensive than everyone else.' He has always held that improving the quality of an event is always worth the money spent on it. This philosophy made weddings the perfect place for Martin and team to be in. Indian families with deep pockets have never spared any expense when it comes to weddings in the family. There were unlimited budgets for ideas and enough money for international florists, caterers from other cities, etc. The first wedding Martin was approached to handle was for a jewellery brand. He made his mark, and since then the team has been handling about three to five large weddings a year for the same communities and in the same circles.

'We used to turn down more briefs than we would take, if we sensed that the brand didn't have the money or couldn't afford us. We have always been more expensive than everyone else.'

Martin and team quickly applied this learning to their corporate work. They started working with brands to do what they called 'special events' — events where the brief is holistic and includes several aspects like a product launch, catering services, housekeeping, ambient experiences, design, etc. He felt that they were more comfortable handling an overall exclusive event experience than managing events that were dominated by a single experience like a product launch with other aspects like F&B thrown in, depending on availability of funds. This is where Martin found himself being able to stand out and do his best, and therefore, he built a reputation on it. Having found his niche, he focused all his energies on luxury brands and complex large format events where his international sensibilities, upbringing and track record helped him score over many others.

VENTURING INTO THE FESTIVAL MARKET

The Live Events industry uses several different names to refer to a single thing without it seeming strange or confusing to anyone! To put this in context, most Indians have a 'proper name' (also referred to as the 'good name', 'school name' or 'real name'). However, we are also called by a different name by our family and close friends. This is our 'pet name'. In a determined effort to defy logic, this 'pet name' has nothing to do either phonetically or semantically with the 'proper name'. So, it is never as simple as an abbreviation of the 'proper name'. I personally have about five pet names, some of which are too embarrassing to utter. True to this very Indian tradition, the live events (or BTL (Below-the-Line) / experiential marketing / brand activations) industry assigns several names to refer to the 'Festivals' market within events. Whether we call it 'Intellectual Property' events (IPs), or 'Festivals', or 'Special Events' this is a new and exciting area of events that promises to be more sustainable than project-based commissioned events.

Festivals are branded events like the Sunburn Music Festival, The Kala Ghoda Festival or the NH7 Weekender that are held periodically and consumers are expected to pay for these rather than be invited by brands to participate. Festivals are about skewing the market towards the consumer and what they want, rather than the needs of a brand. Martin is very keen on building the festival market in India, and is convinced that festivals are the future of live events in the country. He says that the West has already a well-developed festival market. 'Just contrasting Mumbai with London...tonight alone in London there will be about 150 music festivals or concerts, there will be 30 dance performances. Live is huge. Every single person in the UK will spend an average of 50 pounds or INR 5000 each per year on live events.' So while there will be about 500-600 live events happening in London tonight, there will be about 12-15 in Mumbai.

Martin believes that at some point we are going to catch up because we seem to be headed that way. He is certain that corporate event marketing is going to become relatively less important in terms of most agencies' bottom line. About his own agency, Martin notes, 'In about five years time, I would hope that corporate event management would become less than 25% of our business.' It is a bold decision, and he believes that even if he is five years ahead of time, the decision will eventually pay off. He is quick to add that this may not be true of some agencies who want to stick to corporate events as their mainstay, but rather it is the route Martin has decided to take. He admits that, 'It does mean that we are taking a big leap of faith in the Indian consumer and the Indian consumption story, but I think that's a relatively safe bet.' That is the way it has been internationally because Western countries have always (until very recently) seen economic surplus. There has always been a culture of paying for entertainment. That's a culture that we saw in India only in the last four or five years. Things gradually changed and in 2008 and 2009, with the launch of Blue Frog in Mumbai, Sunburn Music Festival and the NH7 Weekender, it looked like the Indian urban middle class was opening up to seeking out and paying for live entertainment. Martin made a decision to get involved in the festival market. He is so convinced that festivals is the way of the future, that in the last three years, these have become 35% of his agency's business. His biggest festivals are India Bike Week and Zumbala — a yoga spirituality festival that he plans to organise pan-India first and then take overseas to the UK and Singapore. The Kala Ghoda Festival has been going on for some years now, and there are more in the pipeline.

HOW WE STACK UP AGAINST GLOBAL LIVE EVENTS

Martin sees himself as one of the premier festival promoters in India. He points out: 'We are still in a generation that needs to buy a house, a car or a fridge before even thinking of going to Goa for a festival. In Europe and America, the business is entirely dominated by promotion: artist promotion, art promotion, festival promotion (or IP events) and management.' The segment that does event management is much smaller. They do experiential work that covers several segments like exhibitions, special events, corporate events, press events, below-the-line activations and several others. However, all the big money and talent is in the promotion business. Martin estimates that we may be roughly 10-20 years behind the developed Western countries in the live events space.

Closer to home, China is somewhat ahead in the developmental path because about six months ago, there were three music festivals in two weeks in Shanghai and Beijing, and between the three of them, they sold about 450,000 tickets of approximately USD 200 each. The most popular Indian electronic dance music festival sells about 20,000-25,000 tickets. There may be some time to go before we catch up, but the market looks promising.

HOW MARTIN MAKES IT WORK

Successful people often say that success cannot be planned. They focus on the principles they want to live and work by, and ironically, the same principles that keep them grounded are the ones that guide them to heights of success earlier considered impossible. Martin comes across as a person who lives by his own rules. He didn't get intimidated or doubt himself when he saw his peers grow in size and their teams grow in numbers. He just went about doing his thing in the only way he knew and at a pace he knew he could pull off.

He runs his small team at Seventy EMG as a 'flat organisation', without much of a hierarchy. Everyone bounces ideas off each other. He makes room for leaders to grow. He feels, 'If you have built a business where you are the most important person there is, then it is a lousy business. So, you need to create an environment where the middle and top management levels feel that they have a stake in the game and that they have the ability to get things changed if they need to. I believe that is how Apple did things.' At the end of the day, Martin echoed what every icon in the creative business believes: 'It's always been about the work. It's always been about how good we can make this (an event), and not about how much money we can make from it.'

'If you have built a business where you are the most important person there is, then it

is a lousy business. So, you need to create an environment where the middle and top management levels feel that they have a stake in the game and that they have the ability to get things changed if they need to. I believe that is how Apple did things.'

Michael Menezes, Owner, Showtime Group

6

FOR THE LOVE OF TECHNOLOGY

With Michael Menezes, ***Showtime***

Let's face it. There are very few parents who are thrilled at the prospect of their children pursuing a career in live events. Though factors like job satisfaction, global travel prospects and attractive pay scales placate their taut nerves somewhat. To be fair to our parents, this is a very understandable sentiment. To borrow a line from our current Prime Minister Narendra Modi, 'Behind affections lie expectations'. We can only do justice to their affections by 'doing well' and living up to their expectations.

Now consider this. Most young bright minds are not keen on pursuing an events career, primarily because of a lack of knowledge. Event agencies, with a turnover of about 100-odd crore or so, pale in comparison to large MNCs with turnovers running into a few thousand crore. Nor are the fruits of our efforts easily available in the public domain for all to see. It is not like a television commercial, that one can catch some 5 times a day. So anyone outside the industry thinks they can safely assume that however broad the definition of 'doing well' may be, event management doesn't fit the bill!

Blame our education system for this. We steadfastly refuse to give events their due. Most often, event management is a part of Mass Communication studies. I mean, mass communication is the most ambitious course on the planet as far as I'm concerned. In two years, they try and cover Media studies, Journalism, Advertising, Audio Visual or Film studies, Events and Public Relations. Phew! There are accredited courses in Europe and the USA that specifically cover only event technology, while in India we think that by doing a mass communication degree, we are limiting our options. Very honestly, for an industry that is so critical in the marketing mix, we do a terrible job of marketing ourselves!

Let us take one important and rapidly growing aspect of events — technology. Now technology is changing the way the world does things. It is changing the way people work; it is changing relationships and the way we connect. Understandably, it is changing the face of events as well. Here are two examples:

1. ***Augmented Reality***: This technology takes a real life three-dimensional scene and superimposes virtual elements on it to create a hybrid view of the real world and the superimposed elements. Let's apply that to a live event scenario like a conference, for example. Imagine being able to view a co-attendee's information including name, organisation, etc., as a pop-up. That totally eliminates the risk of

forgetting someone's face. So much can be done with this to display additional information about products, maps, etc., at an event. To understand this concept better, you can go through several videos online on the subject of augmented reality and its application in events and trade shows.

2. *Wearable Technology*: We have several successful examples of wearable technology that can measure what we do, like the very popular Fitbit Flex band, the Nike Fuel band or the Google Glass. Imagine a technology like this that can monitor our pulse and other factors that monitor physical repercussions of emotional or visual cues. Brands whose products claim to elicit such emotional or visual responses can prove their point live to audiences!

A single chapter is far too small to explore the entire scope of technology in events, but my intention is to point out what a sea change it will bring about. The reasons why people shy away from events can be a thing of the past:

a. *Measurability*: Audience reactions and feedback will make events measurable.
b. *Cost Effectiveness*: Cost per contact of events is much higher than any other communication channel.
c. *Reach:* The reach of events is intrinsically finite, and social media can change things somewhat.

When events become more 'accountable', they are bound to become more desirable. Here is a graphic representation of areas where technology is ready to change the face of events.

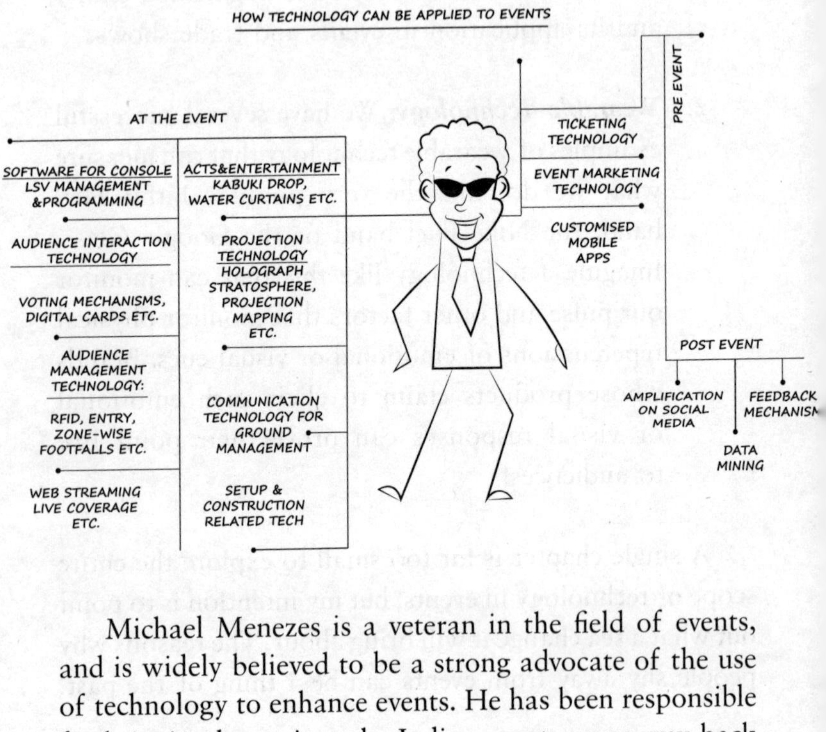

Michael Menezes is a veteran in the field of events, and is widely believed to be a strong advocate of the use of technology to enhance events. He has been responsible for bringing lasers into the Indian events scene way back in 1997. I couldn't have completed this chapter without his thoughts on how technology has shaped events in our country.

Michael Menezes was born in Calicut, Kerala. His journey from the backwaters of Kerala to backstage is full of stories worth a read. He shared glimpses with me that I have put down in this chapter.

His father was in government service, and he moved to Delhi when Michael was just three. He grew up as a 'domesticated north Indian' as he likes to call himself, who was sincere and a good student. He went to the prestigious St. Columba's High School before doing Economics (Honours) in St. Stephen's College. That's exactly the career path my father followed before he moved to England, and I'm told that most upper-middle class Delhi boys of that generation were expected to do the St. Columba's-St. Stephen's Eco route to be considered A-grade students. Don't we just love labels, and stereotypes!

Michael says in retrospect that it was a good thing that he was a good student and usually did well in whatever he tried, because life turned out to be very different from what he planned at almost every step. He started by applying to IIM for Management studies, but ended up making a very naive mistake. He was shortlisted and called for a group-discussion and interview at 9 am. His classmate was called at 9.30, so Michael just assumed that they had communicated the wrong time to him. He happily walked in at 9.30 only to be heavily penalised for the slip-up. That was the first of many life decisions that were made on his behalf by an unusual turn of events.

He landed his first job as a Management trainee with fan and sewing machine major, Usha. As it happened, the two people at Usha in charge of advertising had just quit. The person who replaced them (who was himself shifted into the ad department) picked the unassuming new trainee to assist him. That is how Michael Menezes came to be in the industry that he was to successfully be in for the next 20 years. Fortunately, he loved it and did very well. He quickly moved to DLF from Usha and then to a small ad agency before the entrepreneur in him took the big decision to venture out on his own. He ended up running his own advertising agency called Madhyam for 20 years before his life took another dramatic turn. Michael eventually sold his agency to media giant Publicis and moved on to a career in events.

FINDING HIS TRUE CALLING

Michael explains, 'I was looking for something more exciting in life. I was beginning to get bored.' At this time, which was around 1996, he went for an event technology fair in Singapore. It was there that Michael first saw laser lighting and was very excited at the prospect of bringing the technology to Indian audiences for the first time. Michael imported these lasers and proposed event ideas to many of his corporate clients. He was the typically starry-eyed young agency person and dreamt of a large scale event to celebrate 50 years of Indian Independence. Unfortunately, all his clients turned out to be typically unimaginative eager to thwart agency ideas as overly ambitious and freakishly expensive. They all said it was the government's prerogative to celebrate Independence, and Michael's idea kept being shot down.

Michael Menezes' idea may have been ahead of its time then, but he was convinced that it should see the light of day. His perseverance paid off and eventually, Mr Pawan Munjal, a particularly forward-thinking client, loved the lasers when he saw them and handed Michael a cheque of INR 500,000 to get lasers down to India and do a 36-city tour of events for his brand. Not too many agencies in the 90s saw an upfront client payment of INR 500,000, and Michael's career in events got off to a flying start.

MAKING A CAREER OF EVENTS

Michael believes that because of his background in advertising, a transition to live events was a natural extension. He had spent years working with brands and could talk their language and understand their stories. In events, every new project is a new story with a new client. He wouldn't be tied to a certain client and a single product. Of events he said, 'I thought it had a lot more excitement, but I didn't realise that it had a lot more stress as well.' While creating a commercial, or a design layout, it is possible to step back, change your mind and redo the design or plan a bit. In fact, it is the norm to keep reviewing and making adjustments till the product is near perfection. Live events are very different. When you go live, there are no 're-takes'. An artist either enters stage at exactly the right moment or he doesn't. Similarly, a product-reveal sequence on stage is either timed perfectly to the light and music cues, or it isn't.

Michael Menezes fashioned his career along somewhat similar lines. Once he decided to make a career switch, he sold the advertising agency that he had run successfully for 20 years to start from scratch, and obviously, there was no turning back. He also quickly realised that he was starting off in an industry that almost wasn't one. In the late 90s, live events were unorganised, with very few senior players, and were not even considered an industry within media circles. Michael decided to do his bit to give the industry some shape. He had always been fascinated by technology and decided that it would be his route to create a differentiated offering in live events. Slowly, but surely, he came to be known amongst his peers as the man from whom to expect tech innovations on stage.

WINNING WITH TECHNOLOGY

Lasers hit the Indian stage with Hero Honda, and this opened several doors for Michael, especially within the soon-to-boom automobile market. What followed for Michael and a large part of the Events industry, was the scope to scale up operations. Michael followed up the import of lasers with a few more tech innovations.

Michael's next technological experiment was with Xenon projection: 'A big technology we brought into the country was something called Xenon projection. It was a technology that could project large images on surfaces like walls. Around the same time we brought in projection on water. So we had musical fountains that could be programmed to music, and projected on them. This was in collaboration with a French company. So we constantly looked at bringing in something new.' He then explored more tech innovations and used water projection in several corporate events and launches. In 2003, when he was commissioned to handle the event celebrating 100 years of the Taj Mahal Hotel in India, he used the technology that projected images on water fountains and programmed it to music.

'A big technology we brought into the country (back in 2003) was something called Xenon projection. It was a technology that could project large images on surfaces like walls. Around the same time we brought in projection on water. So we had musical fountains that could be programmed to music, and projected on them.'

One of the things that Prime Minister Narendra Modi's election campaign has been famous for in 2014 is the use of holographic projection to create a 3-dimensional image of Mr Modi that looks as good as real. This technology was brought into India in 2005 by Michael and his team. He used holographic projection technology to re-create Harsha Bhogle and Sanjay Manjrekar in an event where they launched the ICC logo in India for the first time. Michael jokes that Harsha still calls him the 3-D man.

Michael then moved on to 270-degree projection. Up until then, audiences were used to watching images and films on one flat surface (180 degrees). Michael decided to project an image seamlessly on three walls making several events unforgettable for corporate audiences. He soon brought 360-degree projection to his events so that he could project everywhere on the inside of a room or an event venue. Time and again, he stressed on the fact that it was probably not just the technology that helped him create memorable events, but also the application of the technology to ensure that it fits the brand story. For example, he brought in 360-degree projection to launch the Cloud for Tata Consultancy Services, because 360-degree projection is a perfect fit for the concept of the Cloud. He explains, 'We did 360-degree projection for TCS, to launch the Cloud. The technology was a perfect fit for the product and that's what prompted us to suggest it. I believe it is a question of finding the appropriate technology for an event, rather than merely using any novel technology you chance upon.'

Projection mapping was another technology Michael brought in for his shows. Mapping is the ability to project on an uneven surface, in a way that does not distort the projected image or video. So if projection is mapped correctly on a car and a flat surface behind it, then we can give the impression of the car moving against that surface, even if the car is actually still and it's really just the video in the projection that is working. In another example, Michael explained that you can make it seem as if a massive drop of oil is travelling down a building façade or a pillar. The prospects are immense, and several live events and advertising agencies have created stunning experiences for audiences through projection mapping.

CLIENTS WILL BE CLIENTS

Clients are really not as bad as the agency servicing guys make them out to be. Most heads of agencies credit clients by pushing them to explore new acts, innovations and formats in events. After all, every time an act, technology or infrastructure component debuted in the Indian Live Events industry, it is because one client decided to put his money behind it. But there is a downside as well.

Technology is as much of a boon as a bane. There are clients who regularly access YouTube and other video-sharing websites for innovations in events across the globe. Some even put their teams on the job. They often come across interesting technologies that probably cost a million dollars, and ask for a similar effect for a budget of maybe INR 100,000. In some instances, a poor agency guy, who is presented with some such video clip at a meeting with the client, is compelled to sound almost apologetic when admitting that he really cannot create something 'similar' for a very dissimilar budget! Subsequently, the agency representative is compelled to offer a discount on other elements on the event budget-sheet to compensate for his inability to deliver on the client's earlier expectation...of the moon.

While technology is all exciting and cutting-edge, people get bored and expect constant innovations as well. Michael points out, 'Today if you suggest projection mapping to a client, it's possible that he'll ask for an alternative technology because he has seen it used too often at other events. So the challenge is to keep thinking of something new either in technology or its application.'

'Today if you suggest projection mapping to a client, it's possible that he'll ask for an

alternative technology because he has seen it used too often at other events. So the challenge is to keep thinking of something new either in technology or its application.'

MAKING IT LARGE AROUND THE WORLD

Whether it was because of his fascination with technology, which tends to add scale to an idea, or because that is the way he chose to go, Michael ended up doing only large-scale events. He also restricted himself to corporate business because he was comfortable with and understood that space very well. Today, Michael's agency, Showtime, is the global event agency for Infosys. This makes them in-charge of every event they do across the world. When I met Michael, he had just done two events for them in Berlin and Las Vegas. His team has also done several large-scale international events for the Confederation of Indian Industries (CII). Through them, Michael has done events for the World Economic Forum (WEC) and the '60 Years of Indian Independence' in New York for the Government of India.

Michael Menezes has now also ventured into the lucrative IP events space with an event called 'The Jodhpur One World Retreat' — an event instituted by the Maharaja of Jodhpur, in aid of his Indian Head Injury Foundation (IHIF) after his son had a serious injury following a polo accident. This event, that started in 2013, aims to become an annual property.

THE FUTURE

While Michael Menezes has been instrumental in getting several technological innovations to the Indian stage, many other large agencies have fired up event experiences with technology as well. Wizcraft brought in a lot of intelligent lighting; Encompass used the stratosphere to create projection innovations and Cineyug has integrated several high-quality international technology innovations to make TV shows and award nights a visual treat. India has come a long way as far as technology is concerned, but we are still behind the West when it comes to adoption of technology to increase efficiencies in executing events, and that is where the scope lies.

Mohomed Morani, Director, Cineyug Group of Companies

7

STARRY STARRY NIGHTS

With Mohomed Morani, **Cineyug**

At my first job interview, I was asked if I thought a career in live entertainment was glamorous. I was confused when they told me that it's far from that. In hindsight, maybe they meant *I* was not likely to add to the glamour quotient! But let me tell you from all my experience, the Live Events industry is a glamorous, beautiful and creative place to be, though it has its fair share of hard work and long hours.

Just like in the world of film, size, innovation and star power run the show. Off-beat and content-driven events have their place and cater to niche audiences, but most of the money and a lot of the talent are in big shows that stick to the formula. Diversity is the lifeline of any creative medium, but there are some elements that define an industry, and as far as the Live Events industry in India goes, glamour is certainly one of them. But these events come with their share of risks. Big events that feature stars and technology are expensive to execute, and with the threat of economic instability looming over India and the world, brands and entertainment promoters are eager to extend their ROI (Return on Investment). Here are the current trends in the Indian Live Events industry aimed at maximising return on marketing spends and make the effectiveness of events more measurable."

WIDER: Brands and promoters are focussing on reaching wider audiences with ideas that consumers want to engage with. One way to do this is through amplification via allied media. So amplifying an event in digital media, especially through social platforms is gaining ground. With the proliferation of the Internet primarily through mobile devices, social media isn't just a way to reach the classes anymore; they are perfect for reaching the masses as well.

DEEPER: IP events are held periodically, and help go beyond consumer ***engagement***, to build a ***relationship*** with the consumer. Audiences become increasingly loyal to IP events with every passing season and bring their friends in to share the experience. Therefore, the engagement through IP events is far more deep-rooted than stand-alone efforts.

BIGGER: The obvious way to extend the influence of an event is by making it bigger in terms of the content of the show. Stars, unique technology and sheer scale of production are tried and tested elements. The impact and 'wow' factor of such events make them more memorable to audiences.

In an attempt to increase the return on investment and make events more measurable, brands and promoters are eager to extend the influence of events in one of these ways. Here is a graphical representation of how events are scaled up as far as reaching more people is concerned.

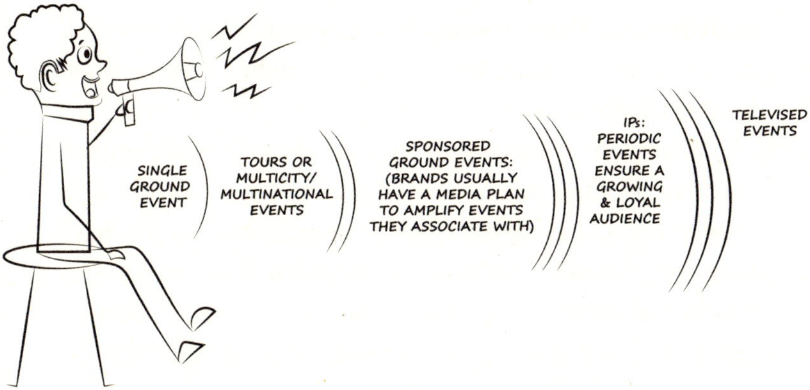

The oldest family in the business of live entertainment in India are the Moranis. They, along with Director Bunty Soorma, built the mega entertainment brand Cineyug. For the last 31 years, they have been setting new benchmarks in large-scale, star-studded and televised events. With expertise ranging all the way from pyrotechnics to film production, the Moranis are big names in both and everything in between. The end-to-end services include concerts, corporate shows, weddings, sports, PR, talent management and production amongst several other things. However, Mohomed Morani has built the Cineyug brand to one of the top names in live entertainment on the back of the unparalleled work done by him in the Televised Events segment where he is believed to be *numero uno*. I had the pleasure of catching up with the charming and very humble Mohomed Morani who is the poetic and creative brain behind all the Cineyug stage shows. He has personally created and directed all the award-winning events and popular television events from the Cineyug stable and has won several national and international awards for his outstanding work. His personal motto is to reach for the stars but never lose sight of the ground beneath his feat.

When Indra Nooyi said that she doesn't think women can have it all, I breathed a sigh of relief. It's normal to expect a busy businessman or a top executive to not have time for grooming or have less time for a social life etc. Mohomed Morani completely bucks the trend. Despite the size of the business he manages and the number of verticals he dabbles in, he looks fitter than the average 25-year-old. I am told he manages to dedicate an hour or two every day to his fitness regime. It was therefore no surprise that he looked completely relaxed as he welcomed me into his office on a busy workday in the upmarket Juhu area of Mumbai. I left somewhat blinded by all the glam and glitter, and wide-eyed by his invaluable insights.

NO SMOKE WITHOUT FIRE

Mohomed Morani grew up in Mumbai as one of four brothers. Morani Fireworks was the family business started by his father. They were the biggest name in pyrotechnics and fireworks in the country and their services included not just firecrackers, but fireworks for business including runway bombs. His father, Mr Gulamali Morani, was a pioneer in the field who started this business way back in 1937. Talking of how it all started, Mohomed Morani explains, 'We started with fireworks and gradually moved into events on a large scale. I personally believe that taking events to television makes the canvas much larger. I would like to take even those events that are not conceived for television, on air because the exposure becomes so much more.'

Mohomed Morani grew up to join his father in the family business, and became trained in pyrotechnics. Morani Fireworks' association with the glamour world started very early. They handled a lot of film pyrotechnics including for films like *Junoon, Zanjeer, Shalimar* back in the 1970s. Ever since, Mohomed Morani was fascinated with this world of entertainment. His brother, Karim Morani, was a good friend of superstar actor Sunny Deol and so Mohomed got to go on the sets of films like *Betaab* etc. It was then that Karim Morani decided that he wanted to make a film. Being in close proximity with the movers and shakers of the film world helped, and Cineyug produced their first film called *Arjun* with very big names from the film industry. Several movies followed and became a part of the business.

THE LURE OF THE STAGE

Does it work to meticulously plan your career years ahead, or do you make the most of what comes your way? Mohomed Morani seems to think that it's a bit of both. While he believes you can never be sure of what the future holds, it is essential that we identify an opportunity when we see one and make the best business decision we can. That is one thing that comes out very clearly through his entire story. His creative mind is always at work, and he has never let an opportunity go by and that is one of the reasons that Cineyug has expanded exponentially in the ecosystem of live events. Here is an incident he related to me.

Mohomed Morani handled the action sequences of the film *Arjun*, and his fascination with the stage kept growing. He remarks, 'I handled the entire action part of the film *Arjun*. At that time, we also ran a boutique of clothes called 'That Man'; under that brand we practically handled the clothes of the entire film industry. So everybody used to make clothes with us — Govinda, Jeetendra, Rakesh Roshan, Dharmendra, Sunny Deol and several others. So as my interaction with the industry grew, so did my fascination, and we started exploring different facets of the industry from a business perspective.' The catalyst for starting events came while on a trip to London. The Morani brothers were travelling with yesteryear actor Dharmendra on that particular trip. The show was very loosely organised with nothing engaging or exciting in the content. This is how he described it: 'There was an orchestra playing. Stars would come, stop the orchestra to say 'Hello' to the audience, then they would deliver some dialogues after which they would get off stage and go away.' This would happen continuously as every half an hour or so, a new star appeared on stage and followed the same routine. For the lack of any other format of shows, even events like these ran to packed audiences with tickets sold out! Mohomed Morani immediately realised he could do much better. Of what crossed his mind then, he reminisces, 'This is fantastic. I want to do a show. Only this time, we will script and cast it and do a film on stage!' He wanted to add soul to live events, like the international musicals he had seen. This is how, in 1989, Mohomed Morani started creating star-studded stage shows as we know them today.

FIND YOUR VOICE

Amongst all the event services that Mohomed Morani and Cineyug have excelled in, one aspect where they are considered to be the very best is televised shows featuring top artists. He has been behind most of the biggest televised stage shows in the country including Filmfare Awards, Zee Cine Awards, Star Screen Awards, Golden Petal Awards for Colors, Star Parivaar Awards etc. In Mohomed Morani's words, 'Eighty-five per cent' of the market share of televised events are ours.'

FORMULA FOR SUCCESS IN TELEVISED EVENTS

Several events professionals work in the space of televised events, but very few have seen success, and no one has seen the level of success Mohomed Morani has. I was keen to know his winning mantra, and he obliged with the story of his experiences.

He talks about ***'Passion'*** for events and the stage as his biggest driver of success. 'We love every day of our work. It's very exciting. If you aren't passionate about an event, you can never do it.' Most creative people say that when you do an inspired piece of work, it reflects on the reaction of the audiences, and as far as Mohomed Morani and his work are concerned, it reflects on his TRPs and awards!

Mohomed Morani also stresses on ***'Research'*** as a critical aspect of creating successful events. He roams the world and does a lot of research because he believes in bringing the best of the world to India and taking the best of India abroad. He has spent the last 30 years directing shows, and strives to make each new show unique.

Lastly, Mohomed Morani strongly believes in ***'Never saying "never".'*** In his words, 'Whatever is not possible to do live on stage is made possible.' In various shows, he has worked around multiple schedules to make artists practise and do stunts and acts that need practice. Just the thought that he wants to do something new drives him, and he tries to get it done despite all possible logistical impediments.

SHOWS THAT HAVE DAZZLED

The first mega stage show he put together was called 'Chamakte Sitare'. He got the star cast of three-four current hit films to come on stage for a magnificent show that ran for a weekend to packed audiences. The stars included Anil Kapoor, Sridevi, Amir Khan, Juhi Chawla, Sanjay Dutt, amongst others. He recounts, 'In 1989, I decided to start creating scripted and directed stage shows. We said let's cast it, direct and script it such that we make a film on stage. Our first attempt was a runaway hit. We opened on a Saturday and it was housefull. Sunday was full too, but more importantly, Monday, despite being a weekday was completely sold out at Wembley Stadium in London. That was the beginning of our journey into live entertainment.' Ever since, there has been no looking back. Mohomed Morani has done about 500 shows with Shah Rukh Khan and about an equal number with Salman Khan and several other big names from Bollywood.

'In 1989, I decided to start creating scripted and directed stage shows. We said let's cast it, direct and script it such that we make a film on stage. Our first attempt was a runaway hit. We opened on a Saturday and it was housefull. Sunday was full too, but more importantly, Monday, despite being a weekday was completely sold out at Wembley Stadium in London. That was the beginning of our journey into live entertainment.'

Mohomed Morani says the key to his leadership in the field of television stage shows is his ability to handle stars and to convince them to put in whatever it takes in terms of their time and physical effort to make the event exactly like he envisages it. He points out, 'Every show is like a movie for us. That is the amount of planning and effort that goes in.'

In the Star Parivaar Awards of 2014, Mohomed Morani directed the show in a way that every star performer had to master a new skill and perform it live on stage. Mohomed Morani got world-renowned magician and inventor Franz Harary to teach TV actor Kunal to perform mind-numbing acts to reveal Star TV's female protagonists live on stage. So determined was Mohomed Morani to get the acts right, that he once sent a trainer to Holland to train one of the actresses who was shooting there for her show. Other performances that needed extensive training included trampoline stunts, fire dances and dangerous stunt sequences that different artists had to spend days rehearsing to perfection. The final reproduction on stage was breathtaking, but it would be, given the task master Mohomed Morani is. Clearly, taking the risk of placing faith on every artist was considered well worth the final output. The only thing Mohomed Morani is scared of is monotony.

In another first, a water stage was created for the Golden Petal Awards. Artists performed by making formations in the water. While Mohomed Morani's direction made the moves look effortless, the artists had to put in long hours to perfect them. In another instance, he used a Kabuki drop to reveal a stage. In the Kabuki system, a large black fabric backdrop held together by magnets disappears in a matter of seconds to reveal an entirely new setup.

Through all his events and televised stage shows, Mohomed Morani has strived to bring in technology and acts that have never been used in India and maybe rarely used elsewhere. The thrill of 'wowing' the audience with new and exciting moments in live shows is what makes his shows what they are.

THE QUEST CONTINUES

One thing common to several very successful people is that they refuse to rest on their laurels. They keep seeking out newer avenues of excellence and expansion. They keep trying to grow personally as well as grow their organisations. Mohomed Morani says, 'We are proud to say that very many of the novel, innovative ideas in the realm of stage shows has been conceived by us. We are continuously on the lookout for how we can grow the industry and ourselves, while offering something new and engaging for audiences.'

One of the drawbacks of the Indian Live Events industry has been the lack of quality indoor venues to conduct large format shows. Very often, when a show of international standards (and Indian proportions) needs to be organised, agencies spend sleepless nights trying to find a suitable venue, and clients spend sleepless nights worrying about how much it will cost them if they have to get a temporary structure made to house such a big event for a large number of people.

The National Sports Club of India (NSCI) is a relatively new and very modern venue in Mumbai that is conducive to large format events, sporting and otherwise. When tenders were invited from companies for managing the venue the whole year round, Mohomed Morani and team pitched to win. By winning the contract, they set a record of sorts by being the first entertainment company to manage and promote a venue of this calibre. The management of NSCI includes conducting events, marketing and brand management. There will be a variety of events conducted at the venue through the year that span sporting events, private and corporate functions, entertainment nights and music gigs.

Mohomed Morani explains about NSCI: 'We don't have a venue like this anywhere in Mumbai. Their advantages are location, capacity and infrastructure to draw in many different events. We have parking spaces, infrastructure, greenrooms, sound, technology etc. As Cineyug, we will leverage our existing clientele and we plan to actively pursue new formats for the operation of NSCI.'

This is certainly a breakthrough in the industry and a step in the right direction for an industry where most business is project-based and has very little long-term stability. Being contracted to manage an international-level venue for as long as 9 years, Cineyug has set the stage for more such deals. Apart from the benefit to the industry, Mohomed Morani and the team at Cineyug stand to gain significantly from this deal. Firstly, they will now have the ability to conduct multiple formats of shows and increase their gamut of experience. The venue lends itself to this because of its size and technical specifications. Secondly, Cineyug aims to create a brand of the venue and will also build their own brand in the process. Lastly, they will now have the option to partner with interesting international and national promoters of unique entertainment projects.

'We don't have a venue like this (NSCI) anywhere in Mumbai. Their advantages are location, capacity and infrastructure to draw in many different events. We have parking spaces, infrastructure, greenrooms, sound, technology etc. As Cineyug, we will leverage our existing clientele and plan to actively pursue new formats for the operation of NSCI.'

THE FUTURE

Mohomed Morani is a man with a vision and a man on a mission. His goal is to change the way people see television. He refuses to bore audiences with repeat content and an overdose of run-of-the-mill dance performances. Mohomed Morani has made the biggest names in Bollywood debut on the live stage, including Deepika Padukone, Katrina Kaif, Shahid Kapoor and Nargis Fakri. When Ranbir Kapoor and Imran Khan expressed their reservations about hosting a popular television award show together, it was Mohomed Morani who managed to finally talk them into it. We now have stars becoming increasingly accessible to audiences and fans because of social media, but this direct connection started way back with the genre of live shows that the Moranis and team at Cineyug made possible. Mohomed Morani now wants team Cineyug to become the face of Bollywood in the world. We certainly wish him the best.

(L-R) Sukrit Singh – CEO, Geometry Global Encompass Network; Sir Martin Sorrell – CEO, WPP Plc; Roshan Abbas – Managing Director, Geometry Global Encompass Network

8

STEAL THE SHOW WITH CREATIVITY

With Roshan Abbas & Sukrit Singh
Geometry Global—Encompass Network

There was a time when an event manager was a mere aggregator. A resourceful hustler would get a set fabricator to put up a stage with a backdrop, get an artist, some technical guys to manage light-sound-video, basic manpower and throw them in together. What emerged was a show. No one was quite sure who pulled it off, but all these people were used to adjusting with each other while rendering their part of the deal for a fixed fee. Needless to say, everyone (especially the client), resented the event manager for what they assumed was a hefty margin he was making despite being the only one in this mix without any talent of his own!

Those were the days, when, if you had seen one event manager, you had seen them all! Pitches were won on cost and there was no loyalty. Business would go the way of the lowest bidder for the event. Things started changing 20-25 years ago. Then, we had our own version of the Renaissance. The Live Events industry faced its most difficult question.

WHAT IS AT OUR CORE?

To my mind, the individuals and agencies that have managed to be true to themselves and have answered this question are the handful that have shaped the Live Events industry in the last two decades. I have represented three winning strategies of this generation.

One of the doyens of the Experiential Marketing industry, who stands by his core competence of CREATIVITY with everything he's got, is Roshan Abbas. He and partner Sukrit Singh are arguably the most creative duo in the Experiential industry today. While Roshan's stories transport the audience to a magical land, Sukrit weaves his magic through stunning visuals and sets. Together, they create magic for brands in the Events industry. I have had the privilege of interviewing them separately while I was writing this book, and came back with quite a story to tell.

They say multi-tasking is a skill that a rare set of leaders have. Roshan Abbas epitomises this trait. He juggles his role at Encompass with various other professional and creative pursuits – which makes his wealth of experience invaluable. There is much to learn from a man who has three day jobs (he runs two agencies and is a part of a group of Angel investors), and is a public figure as a radio jockey, live anchor and film director (and erstwhile TV personality). He also loves to travel, read and cook.

What gives Roshan an edge in events is his unwavering belief that content is truly king. By his own admission, a project can only interest him if it has an idea at the core! Here is what I learnt over a decade in his agency, and a chat while writing this book.

ALL THE WORLD'S A STAGE — A CREATIVE GUIDE TO ACING A SHOW

Roshan Abbas was born in Lucknow to a middle class family. His parents were teachers. He spent his first

17 years there and studied in La Martiniere. As a school-going boy in the 70s, in the small city of Lucknow, all he heard was his friends aspiring towards traditionally respected careers. Some wanted to be doctors, others engineers, or maybe try for the Railway Board. Entrepreneurial ambitions were limited to small-scale businesses like a local tailoring shop. No one had ever heard of a career in the media. But Roshan studied in a forward-thinking school where extra-curricular activities were extremely important. He was a very bright student and got good grades. However, by his own admission, he was much too free-spirited to aspire to be in a regular job. In his words, 'I was a science student looking at the insides of cockroaches and frogs, and not liking it.' Theatre intrigued him from a very young age and he found Shakespeare and the stage a lot more interesting and challenging than anything on the curriculum.

Roshan continued with theatre through his formative years and well into his professional life, and it has influenced everything he has done. When asked why and how events, he says, 'I'm just a guy who keeps looking for a bigger stage and a bigger audience. People say it is limiting to know your boundaries. I completely disagree. I think it's most liberating to know your boundaries, because only then do you know how high you have to jump.'

His love of language and literature spilled over into his career choices. He boasts having covered a chunk of the English alphabet over the last 20 years!

MA — His parents always wanted him to have a Master's degree, so he got an MA in Mass Communication.

MB (A) — He did not do a formal MBA, but has earned it on the job, handling events that have a brand message at the core.

MC — He has been a host on stage for practically all the top brands that could afford him!

MD — He is the Managing Director of Encompass, the Experiential Marketing agency that he set up with his friend and junior from college, Sukrit Singh.

ME — Media Entrepreneur. He is a part of the GSF (Global Superangels Forum) that invests in media start-ups in the digital space.

'People say it is limiting to know your boundaries. I completely disagree. I think it's most liberating to know your boundaries, because only then do you know how high you have to jump.'

THE ROAD NOT TAKEN

Roshan explains why he and partner Sukrit Singh make a winning combination: 'Sukrit is a brilliant artist and visualiser, while I am someone who would rather paint pictures in the mind through stories.' Talking about how Roshan found himself where he is today, he says, 'I think teachers find certain buttons within you very early, and those really make you what you are. I had a teacher called Elton D'Souza who used to often admonish us in Shakespearean terms! I think his sense of playfulness with language, his enjoyment of theatre, all was passed onto me.' Roshan's parents were both teachers, so for them, anything that led you higher up the knowledge tree, was of immense value. Even listening to music and knowing about the song was knowledge, and it was not looked down upon as meaningless entertainment.

Meanwhile, Sukrit too was growing up in a family that appreciated the Arts and Entertainment. His mother was a painter, and Sukrit inherited her creative genes. He loved sketching even as a child, so when he started working with a theatre group as a production person, he took a keen interest in the designers who would create the sets for his group. He saw what they did and was convinced he could do a better job; that's when he became a set designer. Sukrit points out: 'When you use an innate design instinct, the product turns out to be infinitely better.'

Years later, Encompass was born. Roshan did not plan to start an event agency as much as it became a natural progression. Roshan Abbas and Sukrit Singh were both 'talent' rather than talent managers. Public-speaking came very early to Roshan. He hosted shows while Sukrit designed sets and stages. Whenever Roshan was a part of an event as a host, he would try and add value by giving creative ideas. Titbits that could add to the show – a gag here, a game suggestion there, a break in format, and the like. However, he often found that there was a gap between how he had conceptualised the idea, and how it eventually got executed. What was possibly worse was that sometimes he found his ideas being implemented without his permission and consequently, without him being paid anything for it or even being given credit. This happened with both Roshan and Sukrit repeatedly till they decided to take things in their own hands and offer a more complete event experience as an agency. So they started Encompass. What set the agency apart from its very inception was the firm belief of the partners that a creative idea can originate from anyone – as Sukrit says, 'Creativity is not the bastion of the creative team.' They built their agency to ensure that the Client Servicing team are not just paper-pushers; they were groomed to own the creative process and product as much as the creative team.

Sukrit explains: 'Creative' is seen in two aspects – words and visuals. So traditionally, a creative resource in an agency is either a copywriter, artist or visualiser. But, I think in this industry, we are in a unique place. To us, creative is the experience; so it could be the way that experience looks, the way it feels, emotional highs and lows, it could even be the food! So, I believe we can't define "creative" in the traditional restrictive perspective at all.'

Roshan and Sukrit have structured their large team of 560 people along the lines of their philosophy. Sukrit points out: 'We have over 100 clients and our team handles about 1,000 projects a year. So, it's important for us to add method to the inevitable madness. What we have done is put together what we call the Pivotal Team. This is actually a team of planners or creative people (whatever you want to call them), drawn out of everyday event and activation specialisations like servicing, creative and copywriting. They come together to take the brief and convert it into a creative product.' The Pivotal Team is guided by the network's proprietary creative framework called Leonardo, which they adapt to Indian circumstances and client requirements. Sukrit is quick to add that the framework is suggestive and the agency is open to the team evolving their own frameworks as well. These measures make their agency stand out as the only one with an organised, structured creative agenda that converts into bespoke experiences for clients and brand marketers.

Their initial experience of being part of events that seemed to be cobbled together with no compelling storyline, made them agree on one thing from the start – they firmly believed that whatever project they take up should have an idea at the core, and not just be a sum of acts put together on stage. As an agency, they agreed to focus on the application of the knowledge and not just availability.

APPLICATION OVER AVAILABILITY

Here is an award-winning example of what he meant by the application of creativity. One of their clients out of Delhi, the Fortis Healthcare group, wanted to launch a state-of-the-art hospital called FMRI, which they called 'the next generation hospital' that rested on the four pillars of talent, technology, infrastructure and service. The agency decided to use technology as their pillar for the launch event to bring alive this Mecca of healthcare.

The thought was that hospitals don't bring out the most positive emotions, and people do not want to spend time inspecting such a facility. The invitees of the event would be more comfortable in the corridors of power and social soirées. The agency decided to literally tell the story INSIDE OUT! Behind all the high-tech machinery and the brick and mortar, lay the soul of the Fortis Healthcare group. The façade of the hospital became the canvas for the story. As dusk fell on the day of the launch, a video was projected on the façade of the establishment, which became India's largest 100% indigenous surface mapping project that incorporated the beauty of the hardware along with the element of care. The medium and the message spoke one language – 'Touch Tomorrow'.

While the technology in the above example is path-breaking in itself, it is the creative application to suit the requirement of the event and the brand story that won the agency a gold for the 'Best Use of Technology in an Event' at the prestigious EEMAX Awards 2014.

'Creative is seen in two aspects – words and visuals. So traditionally, a creative resource in an agency is either a copywriter, artist or visualiser. But, I think in this industry, we are in a unique place. To us, creative is the experience; so it could be the way that experience looks, the way it feels, emotional highs and lows, it could even be the food! So, I believe we can't define "creative" in the traditional restrictive perspective at all.'

CREATIVITY COMES AT A COST

Roshan says, 'We believed we always wanted to work with brands. We wanted to have a brand conversation.' He believes in using talent, technology and all other elements of an event as a part of one big story. All his events have narratives that bring brands to life.

However, standing up for the sanctity of content and creativity in an event, sometimes even at the cost of monetary gains, has its fair share of heartbreak. Roshan explains: 'While everybody starts at the holy grail of the idea, they all end at the unholy grail of cost. When I see an idea sacrificed to cost, that's the worst feeling I come back with.' While marketers have always argued that cost constraints should not affect the quality of an idea, event managers differ. Sometimes, the only way an idea can come to life is through entertainment, acts, films and technology of a certain standard and calibre. When cost constraints require eliminating some crucial elements, the execution of the idea falls short.

Sukrit also underscores the importance of the idea or creative: 'Events used to be the poor country cousin of advertising, so when people said that creative aims to influence the behaviour of audiences, they meant pictures and words did. I think the Live Events industry does the same, through a different rendition of creative. Pictures and words do change human behaviour, but in our industry, we use experiences that play out in a time-frame, in a particular situation to incite a certain emotion, by making you feel a certain way. So, creative is the final product we deliver which fulfils the objective of influencing opinion.'

KEEPING UP WITH THE SPEED OF LIGHT

Maybe creative does influence opinion. It certainly does make a message more palatable. But for the sake of argument, a fair question to ask is: 'Why do we need to focus on creativity at all? Can we not make a show successful with a really big star or a very entertaining performance?' Roshan believes that we must not restrict ourselves to just that. The newest challenge to our creativity is the current communication scenario. 'The communication wheel in a person's life keeps getting more and more cluttered, so their attention span keeps getting smaller. Therefore, the number of tricks you need to pull out of your hat to engage them keeps going up. You are now planning for a person with a lot less attention span and a lot more means of communication.' Up until a few years ago, one strong act was good enough to see a show through, but that's just not good enough anymore. Creativity in live events is not just about the central idea; it is a thread that runs through every element of the event. It starts even before the event with the invitations and communication that go out to the audience who are expected to attend, and ends only after the event, often with a small parting engagement that stays with the audience / consumer, and the social outreach of the event. The challenge, therefore, is to populate the entire duration of the show with the right mix of engagement ideas. Here too, Roshan's background in theatre stood him in good stead. 'To me this was theatre. Anything being done by a brand on stage was theatre. In theatre, you've learnt every trick. How to engage an audience, how to keep them quiet, how to keep them on the edge of their seats, what should come pre-interval, what should come post, how does Act 1 go into Act 2...etc. I would recommend, anybody who wants to do formatted stage-based events, must do theatre.'

'The communication wheel in a person's life keeps getting more and more cluttered, so their attention span keeps getting smaller. Therefore, the number of tricks you need to pull out of your hat to engage them keeps going up. You are now planning for a person with a lot less attention span and a lot more means of communication.'

THE TIMES THEY ARE A-CHANGING

On what keeps him going, he says, '(in events) No two days are alike. You work with the most diverse set of people...one day, you are talking to a lyricist and a singer and a musician. The next day, you are talking to a dancer, a light man and a technology projectionist...diversity of conversation in events is unmatched.' While talking to all these people, an event manager's mind needs to constantly be at work. The way knowledge has been democratised, everyone has access to artists and talent. There was a time when artist managers kept their access to stars and talent a closely guarded secret. Now, anyone with the time and inclination can figure out a way of directly getting in touch with performers or their secretaries. In this scenario, application trumps availability. It is how the act is played out and integrated in the fabric of the event, rather than the mere performance that makes the difference. And it is this creative application that Roshan cannot stress on enough.

ONCE AN EVENT MANAGER, ALWAYS ONE

While he insists that ideas and communication are his forte and that he is medium-agnostic, Roshan admits that it is his event manager persona that spills over into his daily life. Even when on a holiday with the family, he is the 'go-to' man for everything. He says, 'I will figure everything out. I will figure the bus route, the taxi route, the cheapest route, the most luxurious route...and I will have a contingency and a second contingency!' When talking about his film, he says, 'The times I have succeeded in my films, are the times I have put my "event-brain" to task.

'In events, there is no saying "This can be done tomorrow!" There are no "re-takes" or second chances. We have to have a solution for the moment. So, as an event manager, you have to use your judgement and be willing to let small mistakes fly because of the bigger picture. There is truly no better crisis manager than an event manager.'

Sukrit adds to this by explaining that live experiences have a very small window and one particular setting in which to deliver an experience. 'Yet, we manage to expand the definition of creativity by delivering a multi-sensory product.'

'...the diversity of conversation in events is unmatched.'

NEVER A DULL MOMENT

When Roshan started out in the Live Events industry, he was just learning on the job. It all started with an event for which he landed the contract. The brand was Motorola. Up until then, he had not worked on an entire event for a global brand. The farthest he had gone was piecemeal work for brands like Singer and Gagan Vanaspati. The client had blind faith in him and all Roshan wanted was to prove him right! At that time, Sukrit was fresh out of college. He had just made some films, so Roshan asked him to come on board and design the sets and make the films. That was the beginning of a partnership that culminated with the formation of Encompass, which is today one of the biggest and best corporate event agencies in the industry. Unbelievably, Roshan recounts with a laugh, that the promoters or volunteers (who typically man doors and lend a helping hand backstage) at that Motorola event were Cyrus Sahukar and Samir Kochar! After all, they were 16-year-old kids he could bully because they were in his theatre group.

Importantly, this event made Roshan realise that it was the perfect blend of what he wanted to do. He says, 'I was using my powers of engagement and communication to convert a brand's brief into almost a theatrical production.'

THE BIG DREAM

True to his theatrical leanings, Roshan's big dream is to bring Performing Arts in large formats to India. In his words, 'I can die in peace the day I bring a Cirque du Soleil to India.'

The Cirque du Soleil is an extravagant, proprietary live act by a Canadian company by that name. Described as a dramatic mix of a circus and street entertainment, it is the largest theatrical producer in the world.

Sukrit on the other hand, is realising his dreams by hurtling towards the future in his characteristic style. He dreams of creating the largest experiential network the country has seen, which will have creativity on display at the highest level. He explains how Roshan and he have always wanted to create a team and culture that is both proud of their product, and grounded in mannerisms: 'When a person from the team plots their experience of event execution against a client need and against a creative or design instinct, the outcome is stellar. It takes a little bit of reality, a little of fantasy and some passion, but all of this has to be grounded – then the results will show.'

Sanjoy K Roy, Managing Director, Teamwork Arts

9

THE ARTS, EVENTS AND SOCIAL CHANGE

With Sanjoy K Roy, ***Teamwork Arts***

To my mind, the best way to spend free time is in the pursuit of the arts. Art inspires, unites, and can be an immense source of joy and harmony. Yet, there are very few who nurture this side of themselves, or indulge seriously in any form of art. The sentiment prevalent amongst the average consumer still is that while art is noble, it never made anyone much money — except for the miniscule section of artists who have become celebrities, or those who have combined their artistic skills with good business acumen. Such is the sentiment also about teaching, and several other 'noble' pursuits. But to ignore art as 'unprofitable', is to be short-sighted. The greatest cities of the world are recognised for their arts — Paris for the Louvre, Rome for architecture, Sao Paulo for the Samba, Edinburgh for its festival...the list is unending. And, these cities are increasingly seeing economic activity spurred by the arts.

Closer to home, there have been champions of the arts, who have used its myriad forms to enrich our culture and unite one of the world's most diverse nations. Live events are a platform to bring art to people in an experiential form. Art as entertainment is as old as the business of entertainment. In this context, I spoke at length with Sanjoy K Roy, a visionary event entrepreneur who has not stopped at bringing art alive on stage for people. He is a strong proponent of art as a means to unite a culture deeply divided by economic disparity. As one of the biggest names in the Live Events industry, and certainly one of the few with a truly global reach and impact, Sanjoy has made it his mission to make art the instrument of social change…at scale!

Sanjoy and his team at Teamwork Arts are the brains and brawn behind over 26-odd festivals including the ZEE Jaipur Literature Festival, India by the Bay, Shared History, Kahaani Festival and many more. They describe themselves as a 'highly versatile entertainment company, with roots in the performing arts, social action, and the corporate world'. Teamwork Arts' Managing Director Sanjoy believes in respect for the arts, and the artists. He runs successful events in the performing arts, visual arts and literature across the globe, including in countries like Australia, Canada, Egypt, France, Germany, Hong Kong, Italy, Israel, Korea, Singapore, South Africa, Spain, UK and the USA. Sanjoy has received the National Award for Excellence and Best Director, for the film *Shahjahanabad The Twilight Years*. Notably, he was invited to direct and design the Closing of the Commonwealth Games Arts Festival 2006 – Melbourne & was an advisor to The Kennedy Centre's Maximum India Festival.

HOW CHILDHOOD SHAPES LIFE'S MISSION

Sanjoy K Roy lived about 25 years of his life in Delhi, and the rest in London and Mumbai. His was a small family — his parents and his younger brother. However, there was a big family back home in Kolkata. Sanjoy says, 'All our holidays were spent in Calcutta (as it was called then). All my cousins were there, and I had a huge family on my maternal side. It was a joint family setup, and much of our summer holidays were spent playing "dark room" and pillow fighting.'

The seeds of social change were sowed in Sanjoy's mind way back then. He grew up in a family that was extremely mindful of its responsibility and duty towards the community: 'We have been brought up to be conscious of the fact that we have to give back (to society). Our family has always been deeply involved in doing charity; that included working at the hospitals during wars, running a charitable foundation, or just giving back to the community, etc. In our formative years, we were always told that though we are likely to be in a position of privilege, we must always look beyond ourselves. Even in our home, we always ensured that children of the household help were sent to school and taught at home. They used to call us *bhaiyya* (brother). The environment was always tremendously inclusive; that was natural to us.'

'All our holidays were spent in Calcutta (as it was called then). All my cousins were there, and I had a huge family on my maternal side.

It was a joint family setup, and much of our summer holidays were spent playing "dark room" and pillow fighting.'

Sanjoy's formative years were instrumental in distilling his inclination towards the arts: 'My training has been in the medium of theatre; that has been my semi-professional background. I saw differently-abled children embrace the medium and realised that there is tremendous change one can bring about through the medium of art, or any activity for that matter.'

When asked if his parents were passionate about the arts and whether he had inherited that passion, Sanjoy explains, 'My parents were not particularly keen on the arts, though I believe that all 1.3 billion of us in this country are artistic in our own way. Entertainment is very much a part of every event of our lives. I remember all our driving holidays with our parents were spent singing in the car. So I would say it was a combination of these influences and my own attachment to theatre that really shaped who I am.'

It was, therefore, no surprise when Sanjoy started running the Barry John Theatre Action Group when he was fresh out of college. He remarks, 'We started a children's group called Nukkad, which eventually became the Salaam Baalak Trust. It was a platform for street kids to explore their creative instincts.'

'Entertainment is very much a part of every event of our lives. I remember all our driving

holidays with our parents were spent singing in the car. I would say it was a combination of these influences and my own attachment to theatre that really shaped who I am.'

ON THE ROAD TO SOCIAL INCLUSION

Talking of how it all started, Sanjoy reminisces: 'One of the things that has always driven me is to set up something for social inclusion. Twenty-eight years ago, I set up the Salaam Baalak Trust for street kids—to use the arts as a platform for them to be able to develop their own skill sets and a sense of confidence. Over the years, many of our kids from the Salaam Baalak Trust have gone on to become successful, and primarily it is their work with the arts that has helped them to be able to do that.'

The trust (*www.salaambaalaktrust.com*) was inspired in the 1980s by Meera Nair's film *Salaam Bombay* that revealed the dark underbelly of the life of Mumbai's street children. Sanjoy continues, 'When my kids were growing up, I felt that if my kids could be given the best of everything, including the best schooling, then why couldn't the kids on the street be given similar opportunities?' That was the intent of setting up Salaam Baalak Trust.

In his own field of work — events — Sanjoy infuses the same vision: 'Every event that we do, be it the Jaipur Literature Festival, Kahaani or any other event, we have a programme that reaches out to the marginalised community. So, for example, before the Jaipur Literature Festival, we reached out to 73 schools with about 30,000 kids. These are kids who may not otherwise be able to access a place like the Jaipur Literature Festival because it may be too far or perhaps they just would not feel included. We send our authors out there amongst other things.'

Sanjoy also gives other examples of how the team adds value to the community. The Yuva Ekta Foundation, in association with Sanjoy and his team, produce the Kahaani Festival for children. He says, 'We bring together kids from the mainstream, and kids from semi-urban areas and NGOs in and around Jaipur, to create a street production through workshops and discussions.'

In all this, what keeps Sanjoy most motivated is the effect his efforts have on the lives of the people he reaches out to. He insists on keeping the Jaipur Literature Festival free despite recommendations to the contrary, because he believes that knowledge can bridge the social and economic divides that exist in India. He narrates a touching story from the Jaipur Literature Festival: 'Five years ago, I was receiving people at the JLF (Jaipur Literature Festival), as I do every morning, when I saw this man and a boy who came off the street. They looked like they did not belong, so they were stopped at security. I went up to them and asked, '*Bhaiyya – aap kis kaaran se aaye ho*?' (What brings you here?) The man offered a simple explanation: "I sleep on the footpath outside a hospital and I will never be able to buy my son a book. Nor will I ever be able to send him to school. But I thought that if I get him to hear a story, it could change his life forever. I hear there are stories that are told here at the festival, so I brought him." And that speaks volumes for the success of the festival because it really ticked every box that we could look at. We try to make everything we do, socially inclusive.'

Sanjoy insists on keeping the entry to the Jaipur Literature Festival free despite recommendations to the contrary, because he believes that knowledge can bridge the social and economic divides that exist in India.

THE ROAD TO 'GOOD' IS PAVED WITH OBSTACLES FROM HELL

It is far easier to harbour good intentions than to carry them through. Sanjoy and his team have much to say about what they have had to go through, to make social inclusion a significant reality, at scale. They were busy firming up plans for the Kahaani Festival when they encountered the proverbial '*Kahaani mein* twist'. Says Sanjay, 'The first year we set up Kahaani, we did it in the Maoist belt of Dantewada. That's because we were very keen to walk the talk. Both the Maoists and the government agreed to a ceasefire over the weekend when the kids would gather at the event. We had about 7000 kids from a 100-km radius in and around Dantewada. And the amazing thing was that while we had planned to do Mahabharata, Ramayana and all the epics we had grown up on, the team got there to realise that the reality of those children was very different. They had their own stories about the forest, the stars, the hills and the bears.

They identified with everything around them, but they certainly had no understanding of the Ramayana.' Lessons like these have stood the team in good stead, because as Sanjoy puts it, 'Even launching a product like a car or a toothpaste needs an understanding of the environment, needs sensitivity to social inclusion. It's only when business and the community are perceived as a cohesive whole, that an event can be truly successful.'

'The first year we set up Kahaani, we did it in the Maoist belt of Dantewada. That's because we were very keen to walk the talk. Both the Maoists and the government agreed to a ceasefire over the weekend when the kids would gather at the event. We had about 7000 kids from a 100-km radius in and around Dantewada.'

For those who feel the social impact of art is nearly impossible to measure with any degree of accuracy, or dismiss it as a long-term ideal — Sanjoy has another story to tell. This one is from Johannesburg, South Africa: 'When we set up in South Africa 11 or 12 years ago, one of our principal aims was to bring about development in Newtown (in the South African capital of Johannesburg). The city's economic growth had been completely stalled by crime and violence. Everyone had left the CBD and moved out, and the Johannesburg government was very keen that we did something that would bring back security to the CBD. So we suggested that they demarcate an area so that we could make it an arts district. I promised them that if they could put in good policing and lighting, then we would design the arts district for the community. I promised that if they could deliver, then in three years I would walk across Mary Fitzgerald Square with my laptop exposed and nobody would mug me. That's exactly what has happened now. Restaurants, galleries, photography studios and so much have opened in the arts district. When we started there, we had workshops in Soweto and other dangerous areas, knowing full well what the risks were. But, for those very reasons, I felt there was a need to provide arts as a platform.'

One of Sanjoy's most gripping stories is from a war-torn, strife-ridden country in the west of Asia, bordering Egypt. The team used to host a festival in a university there. Sanjoy narrates, 'The opening ceremony used to be held in an observatory, with glass windows all around. When I got there for the session in the morning, I saw kids in their uniform, holding machine guns. So in my opening address, I half-jokingly said that I would hate to be a professor in that university, given that you can't really argue with a student wielding arms.' The problem, as Sanjoy realised, ran far deeper: 'At the end of the address, two professors got up and said that their students don't have guns. I told them to look outside the window. Guns had become so much a part of their reality that they had even stopped noticing them in the hands of the children!' Sanjoy went on to address the need to ban guns at educational institutions, leading to a section of the citizens prohibiting the use of guns inside educational institutions. This snowballed into a heated discussion where all 36 universities in the country came together and discussed the implications of banning guns at university. As a fallout of the discussions, Sanjoy, as the initiator of the debate was blamed for rocking the boat, and the team had to stop their festival in that part of the world.

In the path to good, you win some, you lose some.

Closer to home, the efforts of Sanjoy and his team paid off in a similarly tough situation. The team had started the 'Sounds of Freedom' festival. They decided to get Bob Geldof, a couple of rappers from Egypt, etc. and put together a show in Delhi. Despite applying for permissions from the administration in Delhi well in advance, two days ahead of the show, their request was turned down. Sanjoy ran from pillar to post, got a historic judgement passed by the acting Chief Justice and secured permissions on the morning of the scheduled event. A lot of damage had been done and the team lost considerable money and a large part of the audience, but it was a valuable lesson in determination. It showed that good could really win over corruption if pursued relentlessly and backed by conviction. As it emerged later, Sanjoy explains, the permissions were denied as payback, by a high-ranking police official whose toes the team had stepped on several years ago!

Sanjoy's several wins and some heartbreaks are all a part of his life's mission to effect social inclusion through the arts; not just in small pockets but as widely as possible. His events include large numbers of people not only across India but in several other countries as well. And he explains that he is able to do this because he does not work for particular brands, he is a promoter of his own events and IPRs (events that are Intellectual Properties, whose rights are held by Teamwork Arts), and so has a free hand in furthering his cause — as he puts it: 'I'm not answerable to anyone.'

About the future, Sanjoy says, 'I think the entertainment industry is the new sunrise industry and more and more people are entering the live events arena. We also have an increasing amount of equity flowing into the entertainment industry. This is why we are now able to see literature festivals across key locations as opposed to nine years ago, when we saw much fewer of these. We have been able to grow from one Jaipur Literature Festival to many more.' He goes on to explain that festivals have always been intrinsically woven into the cultural fabric of society, in all its manifestations. In fact, they have been drivers of the economy, as is apparent during Durga Puja in West Bengal or the Ganesh Chaturthi in Maharashtra. As Sanjoy puts it, 'My intention in more recent times has been to demonstrate that the arts can really create wealth. What is needed now to give a boost to live cultural and art events is for the government to see taxation around such events differently,' says Sanjoy. The Delhi government has already made some headway by introducing the one window-solution to events permissions.

About his own efforts going forward, Sanjoy says, 'Personally, the idea is to continue to grow the space. As long as we are an example of being successful, we hope that many other companies will come into the forefront to do what we do; to work in the arts. We are just one company with 26-odd festivals and events in 42 cities across 16 countries. There is room for many more companies and the scope to reach out to many more countries.'

'My intention in more recent times has been to demonstrate that arts can really create wealth. What is needed now to give a boost to live cultural and art events is for the government to see taxation around such events differently.'

Here's hoping that while Sanjoy and his team have paved the way, several other conscious companies shall follow suit.

Sumit Gandhi (L), Chairman & CEO, Manish Gandhi (R), COO & Executive Director Asian Business Exhibition & Conferences Ltd.

10

THE ROLE OF EXHIBITIONS IN THE EXPERIENTIAL INDUSTRY

With Sumit Gandhi & Manish Gandhi
Asian Business Exhibition & Conferences Ltd

When starry-eyed youngsters on the threshold of their careers, consider a life in 'events', they don't usually pick the exhibition industry. Perceived as a serious, no-frills, business-to-business platform, exhibitions were traditionally viewed as a good business opportunity but with little or no glamour. Moreover, there seemed little scope for creativity when compared to stage shows and other forms of live entertainment.

However, over the last decade or more, the experiential aspect of exhibitions started becoming the focus, and big internationally aware exhibition brands started introducing engagements, activities, entertainment and stars into their shows. As a result, the exhibition industry changed the way business is done. Visual language, entertainment and design thinking became integral to the way businesses interacted with consumers and each other. Today, best-in-class entertainment acts, celebrity endorsers, contests, consumer engagements and creatively designed showcases, are a staple in most world-class exhibition properties. This is the primary reason, a chapter on exhibitions has been included in a book on live events. The story of the evolution of live events cannot sincerely be told without explaining how the paths of the two, events and exhibitions, converged. The shared opportunities for the sectors include an economy that is picking up pace, and the desire of international businesses to enter India. Some key challenges are the lack of infrastructure and the presence of a large number or unorganised players. Unconfirmed industry estimates say that the number of unorganised trade shows in India is 10 times more than the recognised ones. On the infrastructure front, the most pressing need is for quality venues that match global standards.

THE FIRST FAMILY OF EXHIBITIONS IN INDIA

While exploring the evolution and scope of the formidable exhibitions sector in India, I met the biggest indigenous names in the field — Mr Sumit Gandhi, Chairman and CEO of Asian Business Exhibitions & Conferences Ltd (ABEC), and Co-founder Mr Manish Gandhi, COO and Executive Director of ABEC. When I met Mr Sumit Gandhi at his office, my first impression of this successful business magnate and trailblazer in the field of exhibitions, was that he was polite and soft-spoken, but extremely firm and probably a taskmaster. My impression was reinforced when I was directed to his large personal office, because a screen right in front of his huge desk relayed a live video feed from every corner of his establishment. With an eye on everyone at all times, clearly Sumit Gandhi was a man in control of what goes on in his office.

BECOMING A BUSINESS FAMILY

Sumit and Manish's father, the late Mr SM Gandhi was the Founder Chairman of ABEC and a prolific businessman. He started his career as a reporter and eventually went on to become the owner of multiple publications as well as the founder of the very successful exhibition company that his family still runs today, under the watchful guidance of his sons. Sumit says about his early years with his father: 'I was born in Dehradun, and had the privilege of studying in a premier school like Doon Valley. My father was a senior editor; the head of the Garhwal division of Indian Express Group. He later joined the *Times of India*. Growing up around him was exciting because being the head of the Garhwal division, he covered a lot of interesting stories and we heard of them from him. As children, we were, therefore, very blessed to have received the best education there was, and the best journalistic influences from my father's milieu. If there was a big story that he had to cover, or an important event, we as his children would get to accompany him. So we were fortunate to have got exposed to a lot of varied experiences that shaped our personality and broadened our horizons.'

Sumit remembers the family first turned entrepreneurs in 1984-85, when his father started with his own oil and gas publication. Being in touch with the news and players in the sector, the Gandhi family soon, almost unwittingly, forayed into events. Sumit recalls: 'ONGC (the Oil and Natural Gas Corporation Ltd.) was headquartered in Dehradun and they started commissioning small events for things like felicitating a delegate, or making an important announcement around new gas finds, landmark achievements or changes they wanted to publicise. We would end up doing the stories as well as managing the announcement event. That was our first brush with the Events industry.' And there was no turning back.

In 1991, Sumit and Manish's father started the publication of the *Oil Asia Journal* that Sumit explains is the leading journal on the subject till date. As of today, the family holds six publications across different industries including *Oil Asia* and the *A&S magazine*. Of his early years, Sumit recounts that he was initiated into events by fate rather than design, but that he is a perfect fit for the industry. In his own words, 'I am basically a qualified chartered accountant and I keep being asked how I ended up in exhibitions. I see it as finding my own self and discovering my aptitude. I believe in the saying, "Freedom is liking what you do, and doing what you like." I like the feeling of coming to work; that arises from doing things and becoming successful at them. I consider myself fortunate to have "landed up" in exhibitions and eventually to have founded my own in the industry.' Sumit explains that events slowly started growing on the family as publication assignments triggered event enquiries. This led to 'confex' projects which he defined as follows: 'It's known as confex — when there is a mixture of a conference and an exhibition. It is essentially a hybrid where a conference runs with a bit of an exhibition around it. In 2001, we launched our first confex with just about two dozen delegates in Mumbai.' This happened at a time when Sumit was studying in Mumbai and living with his family who had all moved to the city to be with him. Having moved, the Gandhis found themselves in the heart of business and in close proximity to the main ONGC office. Predictably, this resulted in a lot of requests coming in to do events in the style and scale of international formats.

'ONGC was headquartered in Dehradun and they started commissioning small events for things like felicitating a delegate, or making an important announcement around new gas finds, landmark achievements or changes they wanted to publicise. We would end up doing the stories as well as managing the announcement event. That was our first brush with the Events industry.'

CHOOSING A CAREER

Some things, as they say, are meant to be.

Sumit followed up his college degree with a banking stint abroad, but conferences and exhibitions seemed to follow him. He reminisces, 'In 2001, when I was done with college, I considered higher education. However, alongside

I took up a banking job and went for a short stint to Dubai for a course with a company called Schlumberger, which was into smart cards for the oil and gas sector. That's when I ended up seeing a couple of exhibitions in the Dubai World Trade Centre, one of which was a high-end luxury lifestyle show with jewellery, writing instruments and watches. That intrigued me, so when I came back in 2003, I wanted to put together a show like that in our country.'

Manish Gandhi joined his brother in the business in 2002. About his early days in the industry, he elaborates, 'I was working as a logging engineer at Halliburton in Dubai, when I decided to join Sumit in 2002. He had just launched his first exhibition at that time. The first show that I ran was called AV Revolution — a high-end audio-video exhibit. So how we decided to go forward was that he (Sumit) ran his own shows, while I ran my own, both under our company.'

The brothers started building the trade single-mindedly. In all this, what set both Sumit and Manish apart from several other entrepreneurs in the field, was that they had the courage of conviction to see their vision through. From a young age, under the guidance of his family, Sumit decided to grow the business exponentially, rather than organically. This is what has made ABEC possibly the biggest name in indigenous exhibitions today. According to him, 'With our idea in place, we met *The Times of India* and the *Bombay Times* team. We worked out an agreement to do a high-end exhibition called 'Times Glamour'. The first event happened in 2002, and it is still going strong. Today, it has about a hundred-odd exhibitors, happens at a five-star venue and has all the leading jewellers of the country participating.'

AN IDEA SNOWBALLS INTO AN INDUSTRY

Sumit recounts, 'We started our journey with 'Times Glamour', though the Oil and Gas property was already going on. In 2004, we launched education, property and security. We followed it up with architecture and design in 2006. This was followed by more shows, including a travel show, a commercial real estate show, a job fair and a machine tools fair. Today, we do about 62 exhibitions in a year, making us the largest home-made indigenous exhibition company in India.'

The level of detailing that goes into executing an exhibition of global standards is immense and needs large dedicated teams to put in concerted efforts. Sumit elaborates: 'There is a lot that goes into bringing an exhibition to life. It starts with initiating the idea. We then put together a brochure and proposal, develop the design, put the USP in place, calculate the growth potential, identify and sell the show to the right database, outsource the various aspects that need to come together, market and finally manage the entire show.' All these functions are undertaken under the supervision of Sumit, Manish and the team. The founders of ABEC are so confident in their ideas and execution capabilities that they even put their own money into the properties.

The risks are high, but mitigated with foresight and planning. Moreover, that is what makes them the biggest indigenous players in the industry. While explaining the business aspect, Sumit points out, 'Subject to the vision behind properties and the planning that goes in, most exhibitions manage to break even in the first two years. But this is dependent on how the promoters envisage the learning curve of the property. For instance, if you want it to be the *numero uno* event in the industry, then to break even may not suffice. The target in such cases would probably be to establish the property and not try to break even immediately. Here, it is fine to be operating under break-even point for at least two or three years, in an attempt to make it a humungous and formidable event of the industry to the extent that it becomes difficult to omit.'

Manish Gandhi too talks of how they went through the journey and emerged at the very top. 'I started in the industry in 2002 and it's now been 14 years of creating new concepts, developing ideas, marketing and selling them on various platforms. It would be wrong to say that we "targeted" being the biggest. We kept moving ahead and adding portfolios, and now we sell around 150,000 square metres net, making us the largest exhibition company. If I compare this number with a CII (Confederation of Indian Industry), FICCI (Federation of Indian Chambers of Commerce and Industry) or even the auto expo (which is around 70,000 square metres), ACETECH (Architecture Construction Engineering TECH) alone is around 75,000 square metres.'

NOT ALL ROSES

To build a business is tough, but to build a business in an underdeveloped industry is far more challenging. The Gandhis took on the challenges as they came but refused to be slowed down by them. When I asked Sumit why there were so few Indian players in the big league when it comes to exhibitions, he explained. 'It (exhibitions) is a very difficult business to be in. It requires humungous commitment in terms of investment and it is also very service-intensive and hands-on. We have about 300 people in our Mumbai office, 100-odd in Bangaluru and Delhi. So, it takes about 400 people working day-in and day-out to keep our system going and churning out that kind of quality. So, it really is not an easy business.'

Sumit is quick to point out that long-term thinking necessitates distancing promoters from the brand. To keep pace with global players and the way big brands are being developed across the world, the brothers have been careful to ensure that ABEC does not become synonymous with the family name. Sumit says: 'Here (in the experiential industry), many successful examples of properties are promoter-driven. The people behind it represent the brand; they drive it to the extent that the entire brand means very little without them. But, eventually, if you want to build a brand, you need to segregate it from the personality of the promoter. To that extent, brands are difficult to corporatise, but we have been very fortunate for being able to do this and scale it up internationally. Today, our events have global tie-ups with partners across top cities including London. This puts us in the space where we know our teams are global employees, our events are happening across the world and we have offices all over the world.'

'...many successful examples of properties are promoter-driven. The people behind it represent the brand, they drive it to the extent that the entire brand means very little without them. But, eventually, if you want to build a brand, you need to segregate it from the personality of the promoter.'

Manish Gandhi points out: 'What the last five-to-seven years have taught us in terms of uncertainty and recession is that we have to demonstrate a lot of ROI (Return on Investment) to participating brands. So we used to earlier sell exhibition space — which is something that came naturally to us. Now brands want a lot more; they want new concepts and content. They want demonstrable returns. Exhibitions have become increasingly content-driven to answer these needs. We now have speakers who fly in from across the world, workshops and much more. All the new metrics that have now come in, make exhibitions very exciting.'

THE EXHIBITION ECOSYSTEM — STARTING FROM SCRATCH WITH THE ADMINISTRATION AND SUPPLIERS

Sumit and Manish, led by their father, started in this industry from scratch and developed it into the biggest indigenous brand in exhibitions. Manish says, 'I remember in 2002, we closed our financials at INR 25 lakh turnover. Today, we do an annual turnover of around INR 150 crore, with a very healthy profit margin.'

Having been in the business for decades and seen the industry in India grow from scratch, Sumit explains that the industry has come a long way. He remarks, 'Today if we look at the exhibition business, it is quite matured internationally. In India, we are still grappling with infrastructure issues in terms of having world-class exhibition facilities. There is a big event which happens for the Oil and Gas industry in Houston, Texas, called Offshore Technology Conference. My father, ex-chairman of ABEC, used to visit this event, and he got inspired when he saw an execution of this stature, with exhibits spread across several floors and covering an area of 50,000-1,00,000 square metres. There were companies like Halliburton, Schlumberger, British Gas and other such world-class organisations that were participating and presenting papers. He saw how exciting it all was and would come back and discuss it all with us.'

Sumit goes on to explain how he was in his college days when his father shared these ideas, and how it all sounded like a great opportunity. He adds: 'At the same time, the Oil and Gas event that we were handling began growing bigger and the numbers started swelling in terms of delegates. Along with our education, this started becoming very very interesting for us.' The situation of the industry in India was getting better and it was growing well, but as Sumit puts it, 'We travelled along to see these international shows, and made a short holiday of it too. But through all this, the top line and scale of these large global exhibitions made us aspire to bring events of this scale to our country.'

But, as we all know, and as keen businessmen have found out the hard way — it takes more than a dream to bring a big idea to life. Sumit explains how seeing their ideas through took massive efforts involving administrations, suppliers and the whole ecosystem. He says, 'Down the years, we have got very little support from governments. There aren't world-class exhibition venues here even now. Look at Milan, Germany or many other places — they are so far advanced in these respects. Even now when we execute large-scale exhibitions, we grapple with issues like cleaning of the venue, air-conditioning, putting up structures etc. Look at Mumbai for instance, we do not have a set exhibition venue, though there is talk of a Reliance venue in the near future. Even a venue like Pragati Maidan in Delhi needs a facelift. We are talking to the administration through an industry body, and while steps are being taken by them in the right direction, a speedier action plan would definitely help.'

THE FUTURE HOLDS PROMISE

Sumit sees a host of opportunities to expand the exhibition industry and help develop India in ways that are critical for the community. He says, 'The scope for development is immense. India is a completely underdeveloped country in terms of infrastructure, schooling, education and hospitality. The world market is huge and international brands are waking up to the opportunity in India, and heading determinedly in this direction. India is the country that global players are looking up to for the next growth impetus. The signals are positive and the business environment conducive to getting international investments from companies across segments. The opportunities lie in several areas. For example, our infrastructure needs to grow — which calls for investment in the construction sector which will directly impact our events. Compared to the number of exhibitors in shows abroad, there are so many brands that are yet to explore this country. I see that the future holds immense possibilities.'

'The scope for development is immense. India is a completely underdeveloped country in terms of infrastructure, schooling, education and hospitality. The world market is huge and international brands are waking up to the opportunity in India, and heading determinedly in this direction. India is the country that global players are looking up to for the next growth impetus.'

Manish is gung-ho about the future as well. He says, 'We are aggressively looking at more acquisitions in our space, both organically and inorganically. Organically we developed a show called India International Travel and Tourism (IITT) in the travel sector, the healthcare show, and have now planned the finance show and there are some more in the pipeline. Apart from these, we are particularly excited by the start-up culture. I keep going to various forums where I meet a lot of young people who are interested in events and we propagate the idea that if there is a new and innovative concept out there for an event, then we want to fund and develop it to fruition.'

THE STORY OF ACETECH

The number of properties managed and held by the company is too large to be overseen by a single person, so different members of the Gandhi family control different shows. ACETECH is possibly the largest single exhibition property brand under ABEC, and is personally supervised by Sumit Gandhi. In his words, 'Today, ACETECH ranks the third largest in the world in the building materials, design and architecture space.' In fact, according to the official website of the *Economic Times,* ACETECH is Asia's largest exhibition on architecture, construction and design.

Now in its 9th year, ACETECH has grown to yield the highest turnover amongst all of Sumit's exhibition properties. When talking about how it all started he explains, 'We went to Germany, and amongst others, we went to the BAU in Munich. We visited all of these and got inspired. That's when we decided that something like this should happen in India, and we launched our fair here.' The ACETECH exhibition takes place across four cities, Delhi, Mumbai, Bangaluru and Ahmedabad; and has more than 15,35,000 customers. Spread across a massive 42,75,000 square feet, it is a must-visit for the industry.

While explaining how ACETECH has been carefully built as a brand over the years, Sumit explains, 'There are 22 segments in the exhibition including flooring, lighting, air-conditioning, electricals, concrete, kitchens, hardware, glass, ceramics, marble and more. Exhibitors include the biggest brands who want to be visible, including Godrej, Blue Star, Parryware, Roca, Kajaria, Somany and Pidilite amongst others.'

The huge number of loyal visitors of ACETECH includes professionals who are connected with the building and construction industries. Sumit says, 'Architects, designers, interior designers, consultants in the industry, government agencies, hospitality, developers, purchase teams from India and abroad comprise a chunk of the visitors to the ACETECH show every year.' As visitors grow, so does the property. The ABEC team makes sure that the show grows in a new dimension every year, and exhibitors see value in these efforts and keep coming back. As Sumit explains, 'We are now seen as the single-window exhibition property that can help a brand establish itself in this market. Ours is the only platform in which a brand interested in the Indian market can get reactions to their product offerings first-hand from the kind of audience they are targeting.'

ACETECH is more than a straightforward business platform where interested parties transact. Sumit has ensured that the four days of the show are packed with experiences that entertain, engage and involve visitors, and offer more than a product experience. Of one such unique activity at ACETECH, Sumit says, 'For instance, we have an activity called "Design Wall" that gives our exhibitors an opportunity to showcase their most innovative products to a jury. So, two months prior to the show, at a five-star venue, we invite about 100 top-notch architects who are trade visitors. They come in and invite a section of exhibitors whose ideas they find innovative, novel and green-compliant. The final selection of work is showcased at ACETECH to show visitors the best innovations the industry has seen in the past year.'

'We are now seen as the single-window exhibition property that can help a brand establish itself in this market. Ours is the only platform in which a brand interested in the Indian market can get reactions to their product offerings first-hand from the kind of audience they are targeting.'

Sumit goes on to give another example of a buyer-seller meet. In his words, 'Connect (the name given to the buyer-seller meet) is an engagement where we invite all the purchase teams of the developers to meet up with most of our top exhibitors and seal actual deals based on closed-door discussions. Facilitating actual business and seeing deals to their logical end is one of the most fundamental objectives of the show.'

Last year also saw the property pay tribute to Charles Correa, a Padma Vibhushan awardee, for his work as an architect, urban planner and activist. The tribute included an essay competition for students of architecture on how the master architect influenced their realm of design. Besides these engagements, ACETECH has recently launched 'Walk the Talk With Your Mentor', an initiative designed to build a bridge between the young minds in the field and experienced stalwarts.

With the government's initiative to build 100 smart cities in the near future, clubbed with the 'Make in India' initiative, the building and construction industry has plenty to cheer for. ACETECH is in the perfect position to enable this vision by bringing businesses together and providing a platform for international brands to test the waters in the Indian market.

Sumit, Manish and the team at ABEC want to bring the exhibition scenario in India up to speed with the developed countries, and consider this a possibility, given the encouraging rate of growth and conducive business environment of today. Sumit explains: 'We are travelling all over the world and looking at various forums and formats with a view to bringing them to India. There are large shows in Cologne, Germany, Italy and China. We are always on the lookout for new properties and new ideas that we can pick up, invest in and grow ourselves as well as the industry we serve.' Manish adds to this by saying, 'We never go out there and say that we have an exhibition, or a workshop on offer. We always try and understand the objective of the brand in front of us. They may need a social media solution, an outdoor solution or a ground event.

We tackle the exact need of the market by mapping demographics, market realities and all relevant aspects. That is how we deliver ROI.'

With determined efforts by indigenous players and with new talent considering the scope of exhibitions, we hope to see the industry grow exponentially over the next few years.

Vijay Nair, CEO, Only Much Louder

11

THE ROAD NOT TAKEN

With Vijay Nair, ***Only Much Louder***

Advertising is changing with the advent of content in its various forms, cinema is changing with the growing popularity of short films consumed on social media and digital platforms, and reading is changing with bite-sized stories. Inevitably, events are changing too. With consumers demanding entertainment on the go and embracing newer forms of it, event producers are getting the elbow room to explore genres and formats.

WHEN EVENTS DIDN'T CREATE STARS, JUST BORROWED THEM

Most events have traditionally brought big stars from film, music and dance on stage and created live experiences for adoring fans. To get a newcomer on stage and expect audiences to take the trouble of coming to a specific venue, and sometimes even pay for a ticket was absolutely unthinkable. So, event producers naturally hedged their bets by 'borrowing' established stars. Bollywood was one inspiration, but certainly not the only one.

With the advent of multiple screens, consumers started consuming content more frequently and even had the option of content on demand. As consumers started getting exposed to international entertainment and content, they got more exploratory in terms of genres of entertainment. On cue, talent, that earlier considered film, television or even radio as potential launch pads, started considering the live stage. This is especially true of artists exploring non-conventional art forms like Indie-pop, hip-hop, comedy and rock music.

While exploring this subject, I just had to meet the man who was perhaps the first to truly explore different genres of entertainment for live audiences on a big scale. Vijay Nair, who started Only Much Louder (OML), is possibly the most successful event producer to champion all forms of content for stage. He brazenly went ahead with his experimental formats even when he got weary responses from most people around him. Such was his confidence in his idea and the Indian entertainment consumption story, that he did not hesitate to put his money where his mouth was. Today he is the man behind hugely successful live properties like the NH7 Weekender and The Dewarists. While he started off with music, he is fast growing the comedy genre amongst other things in his company.

Not only does Vijay Nair embody everything that new-age entertainment stands for, so does his office in Mumbai's Lower Parel. Just like the alternative entertainment culture that has endeared fans to his events, the office is one of the most offbeat workspaces that you'll find. With very high ceilings and a laid back, colourful atmosphere, it's hard not to want a job there. This, coupled with the open culture where designations have been trashed in favour of teamwork, makes the company even more desirable for youngsters on the lookout for a job that's out of the ordinary. As I was led into an 'un-meeting room', I found myself looking forward to an entirely different perspective on the industry.

OUTSIDE THE DEFINITION

Let me warn you at the very beginning of this chapter that you will probably not get what you started off looking for. Every answer does surprise, but eventually adds up when we see how Vijay Nair's offbeat views have shaped his career, his company and the Live Events industry. His company is behind events and content that has changed the way modern entertainment is viewed in India by a lot of people.

Vijay Nair was born and brought up in Mumbai and embraced the free spirit of the city. He was never one to let others tell him what to do. At the age of 15, fresh out of school and on the threshold of junior college, he started working for an Indie music portal called Gigpad. It was not like he was from a musical family or had any personal talent in the area, but new things never frightened the young man, and he started developing an interest in the business of music. Talking of his stint with Gigpad, Vijay remarks,

'It was a discussion forum for musicians, so that's where I got drawn to working with musicians. Because of them, I knew bands and started working with bands myself. So that happened to me because of the context. I never really grew up listening to music, I was never a "music nerd".'

'It (Vijay Nair's first job in the industry, at Gigpad) was a discussion forum for musicians, so that's where I got drawn to working with musicians. Because of them I knew bands and started working with bands myself. So that happened to me because of the context. I never really grew up listening to music, I was never a "music nerd".'

Vijay's career happened to him when he was busy doing what he loved. He says, 'I dropped out (of Mumbai's Sydenham College of Commerce and Economics) when I was 17 or 18. I was doing commerce, but it didn't make sense to me, so I thought I'd take a year off to do this (music and management of bands).' At first, he did not see this as a long-term option; he took it one year at a time, but before he knew, this became his calling. Vijay always had very sharp instincts and followed through on his hunches to eventually shape a part of the Live Events industry in India.

MAKING EVENT MANAGEMENT A SCALABLE MODEL

After managing bands for a few years, Vijay Nair started exploring the industry. Today, he has built his company to include not just live stage shows, but talent management, online content and content for television. In his opinion, event management needs to move on from where it stands today: 'I see event management as a largely flawed model because at the end of every year, you are back to zero.' This does hold true for most event management companies who work on a project-basis for clients, with no real assurance of repeated business and much less assurance of scaled up business. Of his own business model, Vijay points out, 'We primarily do not operate like an event company, because the way we differentiate ourselves is that we do very little commissioned work. So it's not like clients come and specify what they want and look for agencies to partner them to get it done. Instead, the whole basis of the company is the (entertainment / event) properties that we want to build. We are a very creative company in terms of the fact that the people who work here are really into music and comedy and the things that we do.' Explaining how he selects and pursues properties that he thinks will work, Vijay explains that he and the team travel abroad and keep an eye out for formats that might excite audiences back home. He adds, 'We love building things from scratch. So we'll build and we'll invest our own money into it. We have private equity companies involved with us so we believe in creating and building something that is scalable. Since we start from a particular scale, we know that a fixed number of our events are already going to happen. Then we can keep building newer and newer events over that number.'

Vijay and the team at OML want to explore the genres of art and culture and are fairly certain that they want to keep to that as of now. Like he explains, 'Our mission has been to make sure that the most talented, independent artists anywhere in the country get heard. So every event that we do, be it NH7, Stage42 or anything else that we are building, is keeping that mission in mind. So we have a fairly large cultural agenda that we are trying to push.' He goes on to say that Bollywood is an integral part of India, but while there are many capable event companies out there doing things around Bollywood, the OML team have found their niche outside of the mainstream.

CULTURAL EVENTS CAN SHAPE THE OUTLOOK OF A NATION

Contrary to popular belief that events are born of the local culture, Vijay suggests it may also work the other way round: 'Events shape culture abroad; here we don't yet have those level of events that can shape culture. People don't just suddenly start adopting different trends. It's a process. So, when kids start attending rock concerts, they start listening to rock music a lot more. Or, you start attending stand-up comedy shows, and then start following and watching comedy.' He goes on to say that irrespective of where people come from or whether they are rich or poor, people like to have a good time, and art and culture is very central to that theme. Culture in that aspect covers movies, music, going to the museum and everything in between; the end result is that these experiences enrich life, and this kind of thing happens a lot more abroad.

Vijay believes that culture and events around it have a larger impact on society: 'There is a deep connection between culture and everything that happens in the country, be it politics, GDP or anything else. I think culture is a large part of it. People try and project it as a hobby, but it is not; it is actually a fairly large industry and once people build on it, our industry will really take off.'

Also, when we talk culture, we have to understand that it is pervasive; a culture of a nation is shaped by everyone in society, irrespective of class and demographics. The most successful events are born of and inspired by the culture of the consumers they seek to entertain. Vijay cites an example: 'The concept of Raahgiri in Delhi is beautiful because it's communities organising their own events every Sunday. This should be a national initiative; here it happens as Equal Streets.'

For Vijay and team, a community initiative needs to involve everyone, even the lowest common denominator. Like he says, 'It really can't be just about hip suburban neighbourhoods and Farmers' Markets. It needs to penetrate down to the masses.'

Elitism also exists in other aspects of music and culture. Vijay explains: 'I don't understand elitism in music. Many believe that people who listen to Hindi music are not as 'cool' as those who listen to English music. That is nonsense. In fact, I think it's the other way round because it's impossible to grow up in this country and not like Hindi music. There is enough good Hindi music out there and it's only getting better.'

The reason that Vijay strongly propagates involving everyone is because he sees culture and entertainment as agents of change: 'Music and culture have a huge influence on how people think, probably more than anything else. So the more people are influenced by it, the more we can control our content, and consequently the more liberal and tolerating the society gets.'

Another reality is that live events are mostly created for niche audiences. As Vijay put it, 'Most events, even ours, are primarily built for younger audiences. In fact, not even college students; I would say those in their first or second jobs, between 22 and 35 years. I see that as the kind of audience that is really willing to spend.' He explains that there are not enough events created for families, and he plans to remedy that sometime soon. For consumers of all ages and backgrounds to go for live events, we need a generational shift in the mindset. Vijay says, 'Why are 17-year-olds allowed to go to music festivals and spend money? It's because their parents have done the same, and are happy for their kids to do it. I think this will be the first generation that brings up their children to go out and attend outdoor events.'

Of the immense scope to expand and explore the genre of art and culture live events, Vijay observes, 'You can't expect to catch up with 50 to 60 years of culture abroad in four to five years in India. It will take a lot more time and go to a lot more cities from the current reach in just key cities. So I think it will take some time for the cultural change to happen.'

A LIBERAL CULTURE BEGINS AT HOME

Vijay Nair practises what he preaches. The culture within the organisation is open and breeds creativity. The OML office is large and spacious with high ceilings and unhindered passages. There are about a hundred heads buzzing with ideas at any given time. Here is what Vijay has to say about his company: 'We have always had a very flat hierarchy. We have traditionally never had designations in the company. We just work as different teams. I don't think it makes any difference if you call somebody a "Regional Head" or a "National Head".' Doing away with designations does not lead to doing away with structure and efficiencies. The OML team is about a 100-strong, with a good layer of secondary management. So, each team is divided according to the role they play and every team has a head. This 'alternative' thinking also makes it easier for ideas to flow. Vijay explains: 'We do a lot of workshops in the company. If there are a hundred people, we put together ten teams of ten each and give them the task of coming up with new properties. One of our best ideas 'Stage42' came up like that.' He adds, 'Typically, the idea of a festival comes from somewhere, then there is a creative team that takes over, but we all sit together.' At OML, there are different departments like the design team, the video team and other departments that work together like a well-oiled machine to make an idea concrete. Vijay and the team are comfortable working on a lean model. He points out, 'Our production team is largely just seven or eight people, but during the festivals, there are about 300 to 350 people around, so we have agencies help with the ground production, and some others who help with stage management and other aspects. So, we work a lot with the freelance model networks.' When asked what kind of people would fit right into the culture of his company, Vijay says, 'I would like to have people who are unafraid to speak in terms of the kind of ideas they have. Secondly, I also try and bring in as many fresh people as possible, whose outlook has not yet been messed up by the industry already. The idea is to get people who are really creative and weird; those who will come up with really absurd ideas because that's where the best ideas come from; those who aren't thinking like a box or trying to come up with a branded solution.' Expectedly their hiring process is entirely different from the rest of the industry. Vijay believes, 'We've never looked at anybody's resume because it doesn't make any difference to us. I don't think resumes make any difference in this industry in general. There's nothing in events that needs training. I think there are a lot of people who are born with the skill of being able to put things together. That is all that you really need.'

'The idea is to get people who are really creative and weird; those who will come up with really absurd ideas because that's where the best ideas come from.'

His unconventional views spill over to women's issues as well. Vijay unflinchingly quips, 'In this industry women are at least at par if not higher in terms of capabilities. Despite this, we are an extremely male-dominated patriarchal industry. In our office, half, if not more, are women. To begin with, they are great at organising and they get less stressed than men in most situations. That's a great advantage in this industry.'

SO, WHAT COMPRISES CULTURE AND MUSIC-BASED EVENTS?

With almost two decades of working with music, Vijay has a keen sense of the trends that will shape the future: 'If you take music, Bollywood is the mainstream form of music, then you have independent rock by the likes of Indian Ocean, Raghu Dixit and so on. A level under that would be English rock bands and really under that would be hip-hop, which is an emerging sub-culture. In about two-and-a-half years, I think hip-hop will be one of the biggest sub-cultures in India because the one thing that hip-hop is doing in India that nothing else has managed to do is that hip-hop is emerging from the slums of the country. It is emerging from the most marginalised classes in huge numbers. Once that takes off and we get our first few stars from there, it will be an absolute revolution at the grassroot level.' Vijay goes on to say that there is a separate division in his company now focused on developing talent from this segment, a segment that has typically 'not been exposed to the culture that you and I have.' Their cultural exposure has primarily been restricted to festival times like Diwali, or Ganpati, and the stray fancy dress competitions.

'Hip-hop is an emerging sub-culture. In about two-and-a-half years I think it will be one of the biggest sub-cultures in India, because the one thing that hip-hop is doing in India that nothing else has managed to do, is that hip-hop is emerging from the slums of the country. It is emerging from the most marginalised classes in huge numbers. Once that takes off and we get our first few stars from there, it will be an absolute revolution at the grassroot level.'

Music is where he started, but Vijay insists, 'Our affinity is towards alternative culture, not music. We have already got into comedy and content.' Talking of all the cultural events he has planned, he remarks, 'I think music and comedy are predominant, but dance is something we are going to get into in a fairly big way in the next couple of years. Theatre is something else that we are considering; we started exploring it with 'Stage42', but it's something we still have to wrap our brains around in terms of how to really get into that. But largely, when we think of streams, it would be music, comedy, theatre, dance and movies. These would be the five properties you can build things around; of these, the focus is on music and comedy for us right now.'

EXPLORING NEW GENRES PRESUPPOSES FINDING GREAT TALENT IN THOSE AREAS

While trying newer formats of live entertainment, one would imagine that a company needs to start from scratch. From identifying a market for the genre, to putting together the team of performers and managers who can make the show happen, innovation needs time and instinct. Vijay Nair seems to have it all together in this area too: 'It's not all that difficult for us to find talent. We have a reputation by now. We have done 170-odd international acts in the last five years because of which all the agents and managers know us. So, it's really not a challenge anymore. With the right kind of money and the right kind of approach, you can get the right talent.' Vijay continues to add that with a large team of artist managers in the country, there is a constant flow of fresh talent from within India coming to them: 'Because we have NH7 (OML's hugely popular multi-city music festival), typically everyone will reach out to us — so we have a large pool of talent there itself.'

THE NH7 WEEKENDER — A TRAILBLAZER IN SUCCESSFUL IP CREATION

The now iconic NH7 Weekender is a pioneering music festival in India, conceptualised and managed very successfully by Vijay Nair and the OML team. The first edition took place in 2010 and it has been growing in size and reach ever since. NH7 started six or seven years into OML's operations, now a 13-year-old company, shortly after the company got funding and was able to expand and explore possibilities in the live cultural events space. As Vijay explains, 'We were doing much larger properties and we needed the money to be able to do what we wanted.'

Vijay says of NH7 Weekender, 'It is a classic international music festival format with multiple stages and multiple genres of music. People come and pay for one ticket and the wristband they get lets them go and watch whatever they want. What we have managed to do very successfully is adapt it to India really well. So we had a heavy metal band playing on one stage while Shubha Mudgal sang on another. I think we realised that most people in India listen to all kinds of music. They listen to whatever they like. The same audience listens to electronic music, Sufi music, *Coke Studio* as well as rock songs. So our structure was built around this insight and it worked well.' According to Vijay, what NH7 managed to do for the music consumption milieu was that it exposed music fans to such a format (multiple genres of music apart from the mainstream) and over time it showed the industry that a format like this could work. Vijay says, 'After that, there have been multiple replicas in terms of music festivals. A lot of them started but shut down too, but I think it gave people hope that something like this could happen.'

Of how this idea came to Vijay he says, 'It's (similar formats of music festivals) been happening in the world since Woodstock (The Woodstock Music & Art Fair) happened. For me Glastonbury (The Glastonbury Festival) was a major influence in terms of going there and seeing it for myself. It was the first big music festival I had been to, and I came back and decided that this is what I wanted to do.'

'I think we realised that most people in India listen to all kinds of music. They listen to whatever they like. The same audience listens to electronic music, Sufi music, Coke Studio *as well as rock songs. So our structure (for the NH7 Weekender festival) was built around this insight and it worked well.'*

Apart from an excellent format that makes the NH7 Weekender so endearing to its fans, strong sponsorship is critical to the success of the festival. Vijay says the OML team has this part down pat: 'OML works very differently; we are really good with sponsorships. We are very loyal when it comes to our brands and so are they with us. We have never left brands and they have never left us; so Bacardi has been the sponsor since year one and they still are. Red Bull, Pepsi, Dewar's and others really see this as a long-term deal. So Bacardi will be an eight-year deal; we do not go negotiating year on year. It's a pretty solid proposition once and for all.'

Vijay does say that this kind of firm trust takes time and effort to build, but the team has managed it. When Bacardi first decided to sponsor the festival, both sides were testing the waters: 'It was a standard contract, where the sponsor comes in for a year and has the first right of refusal for the next year. Though the first year, the festival was small, both the sponsor and we could feel that it had potential and could get big. The second year was really big, and after that there was no looking back. We extended it to a long-term deal and we were more than happy the way it turned out.'

Since its cautious beginnings, NH7 has come a really long way on the back of expert planning and foresight. While the event has grown in size, the big achievement has been the fact that it has managed to reach a much wider audience in terms of the number of cities it is present in. Today the festival is held in almost every zone in the country — in Pune (West), Delhi (North), Bangaluru (South), Kolkata (East) and Shillong (North-East). Vijay elaborates, 'It is now a five-city event and I don't think anyone else has dared to try this kind of a property at this scale. Our headliners have got bigger, our acts have got bigger and we have had over 350 to 400 acts played over festivals. NH7 has turned into an iconic property in the sense that it has almost become like a "rite of passage" to play at NH7 and be acknowledged there.'

'When it started out, the festival sold about 2000-odd tickets, according to Vijay's estimates. Today, he says NH7 sells about 20,000 tickets a day. Vijay says, 'Probably only Sunburn and we sell tickets in these number for a music festival in India.' When asked how these numbers stack up against international music festival ticket figures, Vijay says, 'A 20,000-ticket festival would be a mid-range festival. Abroad, there are festivals that sell about 10,000 to 12,000 tickets, that is followed by the 20,000 to 40,000 range and finally there are those that are in the 80,000 to

100,000. But several of these really large festivals that do 100,000 tickets have been happening for 25 to 30 years. By that point of time, we will cross those numbers.' What makes NH7 the runaway success that it is, is clearly the vision of the founders and their constant endeavour to better the experience and reach out to wider audiences. Vijay explains, 'We wanted an NH7 which is accessible within 24 hours from any part of the country, where people can just drive to and reach. That is what we are really aspiring to.'

NH7 has turned into an iconic property in the sense that it has almost become like a "rite of passage" to play at NH7 and be acknowledged there.'

MAINSTREAMING THE ALTERNATE

Vijay refuses to stay put. He's planning the future and it looks like alternate will go mainstream sooner than later if his upcoming projects go the NH7 way. Of his near future plans he says, 'We are starting two new festival properties this year, with a third one in the pipeline. One is an existing format — a conference for the creative industry. With 17 conferences planned for 4000 people, we are trying to bring every single entrepreneur who works in the creative industry, which has 17 different streams, together in one place. This aims to be the biggest creative conference there is.' In terms of the format, he observes, 'It will end as a festival. The conference will end at about five and then there will be gigs all over the city.' Vijay goes on to talk about another property slated for release in the next few months: 'This will be only for families who have kids under the age of 15. The idea is to give families the option to go outdoor.' Vijay promises that there will be programming for mothers, programming for fathers and programming for kids, ensuring that it will be a wholesome family entertainer. In his own words: 'Our next property will be like an NH7 for kids.'

Vinit Karnik, Business Head, ESP Properties

12

LIVE ENTERTAINMENT IS SERIOUS BUSINESS

*With Vinit Karnik, **ESP Properties***

Now let us all come back down to Earth and talk business. Does any of this live entertainment brouhaha even make business sense?

Event managers pride themselves on being experts of *jugaad* (the ability to get seemingly difficult tasks done, with panache). 'Hustler' is the best English translation I can think of, but it doesn't come close to the respect commanded by the term *jugaad* in event circles. Anyway, because of this particular attribute, event managers rarely feel like fish out of water. However, one way to ruffle the feathers of this cool high-flyer is by talking sponsorship.

Monetising events and event properties is just not something even the most seasoned professional is comfortable with. It is one thing to ***spend money*** (albeit effectively) on an event to make it impactful, but quite another to ***make money*** off it. Making a profitable venture out of an event needs the mindset of a shrewd investor with a vision, a risk appetite and sometimes — deep pockets. The hottest brains in the business break into a cold sweat when asked by hard-nosed and savvy brand marketers about ROI (Return on Investment) and other pertinent questions before deciding to sign on as sponsors. The reason these questions are so difficult to answer is that brands that have been sponsoring TV programmes and advertising on traditional media for decades are used to evaluating those spends against their impact on the brand's bottom line. Naturally, metrics such as ROI become their yardstick and sponsorship efforts in new avenues like merchandising, sports properties and ground events need to demonstrate how they stack up against traditional areas of marketing and sponsorship.

This is an area where live ground events is sorely lacking. The only calculation that the industry has come up with is the over-simplified (and highly inaccurate) formula of dividing the money spent by the number of attendees, resulting in an exorbitant cost per contact. The fact that these contacts are heavily engaged in the experience has so far not been quantified, resulting in the 'quality of contact' that is largely unaccounted for. The depth of involvement offered by a live experience at an event just cannot be equated with a 30-second piece of communication with a contact who may have been dozing off with the television switched on (for all we know).

If we see live events entering the big league in the near future with segments like IP events leading growth, then it is imperative to get comfortable with the marketing aspects of an event. The reach of an event is far wider than the square feet area on which it stands. Pressing concerns like these and many more were easily explained by the delightful and extremely humble big shot of the event marketing space, Vinit Karnik, in my chat with him one morning.

When I first spoke to Vinit Karnik on the phone, he heard me out before answering in a warm booming voice that he would love to meet and discuss the book. He was patient, articulate and encouraging, exactly what you would expect the friendly neighbourhood live events professional to be. Except, he's not. He is instead, a globally respected and much quoted authority on the business of live events, with all the humility of the boy next door. I met him shortly after, for his views on everything experiential including entertainment, sports and partnerships.

EARLY YEARS

Vinit Karnik is a classic 'Mumbaikar', complete with a Bachelor's in Commerce. When asked how he landed up in media, he explains that through his growing up years, he was always fascinated by the media, especially from the lens of the audience. He constantly observed how people consumed media and what they liked spending time with. Vinit started his career in the mid 90s when Indian viewers had just two or three channels to choose from, and has remained a (very vocal) spectator through three eras of media consumption, now finding himself in the middle of a boom with over 600 channels in the market. The career path he went on to follow facilitated understanding this aspect of the consumer from very different standpoints. His first job was with the *Times of India*. Now, it is imperative to understand that the *Times of India* (fondly known in media circles as TOI) is the 'Pearly Gates' to the media industry. The media Goliath has been the training / breeding ground of practically every media doyen during their wide-eyed management trainee days. So, Vinit Karnik started in the Times Television division, handling media sales. From there, he moved to a job in media planning and buying. His next stop was a print media job before he decided to join a film production house to co-produce movies. From there, he tried his hand for a short while, at post production and visual effects. In his words, 'Effectively, if you put all I have done in perspective, everything contributed to understanding the mammoth subject called "the media", while continuously changing the lens according to the assignment currently at hand.'

ENTERTAINMENT, ENTERTAINMENT, ENTERTAINMENT

With this background, Vinit understood the entire gamut of media. From the basics of the print media and the essence of planning and buying, he moved to the bigger pie that was entertainment and Bollywood. His stint at Prasad Labs gave him the experience he needed to understand film financing in terms of how to deliver a film ultimately to the exhibitor. If you understand the core, changing perspectives is not a problem. You have to value every perspective to have a meaningful one of your own. My chat with Vinit Karnik taught me to look at events from the consumer's perspective. Event companies traditionally focus on what brands want, while brands focus on what consumers want. It is, therefore, only logical to start with the consumer if we want to understand the whole ecosystem of entertainment. He said during our chat that 'Back in 2003-2004, what entertainment meant to us all was Bollywood movies and movies from the South Indian film industries...basically movies'. At a time when the words 'entertainment' and 'movies' were used almost interchangeably, Broadmind (now known as Mindshare ESP) realised that there was a huge potential for 'branded entertainment' by helping brands to leverage the platform of Bollywood and movies to engage with their consumers.

ENTERTAINMENT MARRIES SPORTS

The gamut of entertainment has now expanded to include sports as a form of entertainment. This unlikely marriage happened because the cricket IPL came about and flung all conventions right out of the grounds with a resounding six. Frankly, it had to be cricket that ushered a revolution in consumption patterns, because up until just a few years ago, we were a one-sport nation. The Board of Control for Cricket in India (BCCI), and perhaps the ICC (International Cricket Council), was the last word in cricket and the business milieu around the sport. This was till 2008 when IPL 'happened' to India. At this time, because Vinit Karnik and the team at Mindshare

ESP spotted the opportunity, 'Because we understood the business, and because we understood the brand side of the story, we were involved with IPL from day 1.' The team was quick to realise that the game would no longer be just about the BCCI or the rights holder, but would have other stakeholders, like the franchisees or the players. So, while Bollywood marketing efforts had some depth by way of appearances, endorsements, shows and the like, sports had a very limited scope. This was the gap that presented itself. Vinit credits this realisation completely to the IPL. IPL was as much about the spectacle as it was about the sport. It was an immersive experience that served to broaden the viewer base of cricket like no one could have imagined. Today, consumers have come to see sports as entertainment as well. Somewhere the lines have blurred between sport and entertainment, resulting in marketing professionals viewing sport from an entirely different perspective, a perspective brought about by the consumers' acceptance of sports as entertainment. Sports has got a new identity and a new benefit. While it has been started by cricket through the IPL, the effects have snowballed and now touch *kabaddi*, tennis and football with varying levels of success. Says Vinit, 'From a sporting perspective, between the 2008-2014 window, we now have between 200 and 300 players in the entire ecosystem, including franchise owners, right holders, associations and even talent, to be able to be in touch with (for marketing initiatives).' Clearly, we now have a whole lot more avenues to monetise sport.

ENTERTAINMENT MARRIES SPORTS, MARRIES LIVE EVENTS

Live entertainment became the next frontier in this happy mix, according to Vinit Karnik. It all started with consumers viewing only Bollywood or movies as the primary source of entertainment. With the IPL (and other subsequent sporting leagues), sports started making its mark as a 'family entertainer' for the first time. Upon closer scrutiny, what emerged was that it was the live aspects of the IPL that were significant in making it an entertainment potboiler. People had started looking forward to matches in their cities and were keen to get a piece of the action live in the stadium. Branding, live music, mascots, celebrities and cheerleaders all contributed to this live experience and atmosphere. It was sometime at this point that the entertainment ecosystem started including and focusing on live events. The need of the hour was to make an event of everything in order to catch the attention of the restless consumer.

It was in 2011-2012 that Vinit and the team decided to build a business ecosystem around live events, similar to that of the far more established film industry and the relatively new Sports Events industry. In the live events space, award shows had some traction amongst consumers, but only because of the television telecast. Every IP owner or rights-holder struggled to sell a sponsorship for an on-ground event. This threw up some immediate requirements.

HOW TO WORK ON AN EVENT AS A BUSINESS PROPOSITION

When considering an event sponsorship proposal, according to Vinit, 'Not many (clients) were biting the bullet, and even if they were, it was from a relationship standpoint.' The obvious first question on a client's mind is: 'Why should I spend a chunk of my money on a one-evening wonder, when I can spread those budgets out over two weeks in traditional media channels?' The following points are an endeavour to answer this concern:

a. ***Measurement Metrics:*** When we look to monetise live events, we add a stakeholder (or a few) to the mix. That means a couple of more opinions around the same event. Vinit says it is important for the rights-holder to be willing to work in a way that accommodates brands. So, if the IP owner or rights-holder is charging an amount from a brand, then what ROI the brand is getting for the amount, will be a concern of every serious brand who is considering long-term sponsorship in the business. To cater to this crucial question, the team at Mindshare evolved a measurement system that would effectively convey to the brand exactly why an event sponsorship proposal would make sense for the brand. This involves explaining to the brand that they are reaching not only a finite number of people present at the event but a quantifiable increment who are keen followers of the event. This means tracking numbers on consumer trends. As Vinit points out, 'We need to tell brands that this is actually an efficient way of investing because people are following this business. People are following these trends; they want to know who won the "Femina Miss India" or the "Filmfare Awards" or even what happened at IIFA in Tampa.' This led Vinit Karnik and team to develop a measurement matrix for live events. He explains, 'Whether it is a sporting property, a live event or a music concert, we have cracked a method which possibly gives you a heads-up for live events measurement.' This measurement system is effective because it has multiple filters. One simple filter is the number of people who experience the event live on ground. But, as Vinit says, 'That's not the big one.' He says that most on-ground consumer events today have a television or broadcast leg. So, there is scope for extrapolating that to TV GRPs (Gross Rating Points). There is also scope for seeing what happens to that event when it is broadcast with or without FCT (Free Commercial Time) etc. In effect, a live event does get amplified beyond its physical boundaries, and there is sense in measuring its impact with a view to packaging events for brand sponsorships.

b. ***Return on Investment (ROI) Versus Return on Objectives (ROO):*** Brand managers look at the scale and scope of an event and evaluate the money they are paying for that scale and scope. This can be measured by two parameters, according to Vinit Karnik — ROI and ROO. In larger events, brands usually look at ROI, because there is scale, marketing, television, etc. involved. Basically, there is enough hoopla around the event that extends its life cycle and influence. However, niche events cannot always be looked at from an investment-driven perspective simply because the numbers would not immediately make business sense from a cost-per-contact angle. For brands, the value of such an event is often delivered via meeting the perfect target audience. For instance, if a brand wants to specifically reach out to 500 consumers in the income bracket of INR 500 crore+, and finds an event that can facilitate just that, then the brand would view such a platform as invaluable, and would not waste time on evaluating cost per contact. The focus of brand managers would then be to calculate ROO. Considering the event delivered for the brand a captive (and perfectly mapped) target audience and their undivided attention for two hours, ROO scores are bound to be high.

c. ***Packaging and Infrastructure:*** The packaging of an experience is a non-negotiable deliverable. People go to cinema halls to watch a film because of the experience of seeing it on a 70mm screen. This experience well outweighs the trouble of getting out of the house, driving all the way to a location and spending money, all for that experience. Tragically, experiences lose their sheen pretty quickly and so need to be constantly packaged and upgraded. So film viewership in single-screen halls fell rapidly before multiplexes came up and upped the experience by delivering orders to seats, improving seat comfort, sound quality, etc. Infrastructure plays an equally crucial role. Badly managed peripherals of an event like washroom facilities, parking, ticketing and entry management systems are significant enough to influence the audience to give up on even a fairly promising event experience.

d. ***Know Your Business Model:*** When an IP owner sets out to market the event, 'He must first ask himself, who is this IP for? Is the business model around sponsorship or subscription?' says Vinit Karnik. He takes the popular electronic dance festival Sunburn as an example. That is an IP whose primary revenue model is subscription. That does not mean that they don't want sponsors; just that they expect to drive and make their money out of selling tickets. The point Vinit makes is that not every IP is conducive to a sponsorship model. Every event does not need to be modelled to have a sponsor. If the product is strong enough, and has established acceptance, audience and subscription can well drive revenue.

One such example is theatre, where the low cost production and frequency of shows easily cover cost via ticket sales. Events like award shows that go on television and have a larger scale appeal to sponsors more easily and lend themselves to marketing.

e. *Accountability and Transparency:* On the whole, the Live Events industry is very guarded about back-end operations. This includes much more than trade secrets like creative ideas. They keep their cards close to their chest, whether it comes to their contacts, cost of execution or source of material and manpower. This is because, a lack of regulatory framework, makes it easy to 'steal' ideas, contacts and concepts if one manages to gain access. When it comes to creating event IPs, the scale and resources required to replicate such events make it far more difficult for competitors to hijack. This is where IP event right holders can relax their guard. But, old habits die hard, and this makes it difficult for brands and media agencies to get a realistic grip of numbers (actual costs, reach, etc.) that are delivered by these events. Vinit Karnik speaks from a media and event marketing practitioner's perspective when he remarks, 'They need to be accountable, they need to be transparent, and they need to be playing a long-term valuation game. They can't expect to launch an event today and make money by selling the event in the next three years for a huge profit. Whoever is willing to go the distance with this will succeed in the long run.'

'They (IP owners) need to be accountable, transparent, and they need to be playing a long-term valuation game. They can't expect to launch an event today and make money by selling the event in the next three years for a huge profit. Whoever is willing to go the distance with this will succeed in the long run.'

f. ***Do Numbers Trump Ideas?:*** When asked if he is one of the few Events industry people who is comfortable with numbers, Vinit Karnik observes, 'I am a numbers person if required, but it's also about articulating numbers when there really aren't any!' He explains that data on live events is not always readily available, but the requirement to quantify is a constant. So what do we do if there is no equivalent of TAM (Television Audience Measurement) data? The solution is quite simply to find a starting point by assuming some numbers based on informed sources. This can eventually become a tool. Vinit explains, 'Even at GroupM, at one point of time, there was nothing on sports or entertainment. How would we evaluate a movie? So, we started something called "Movie Rating Points" which was based on soft data. Producers and directors were rated on people's opinions.

This was then used to evaluate upcoming releases based on who's directing or producing them.' He thinks a similar model would work for the live events space. 'Creating numbers to possibly suit a new or sunrise industry and thereby creating some tools around it, would be something that will ultimately be appreciated from a brand perspective and eventually effectively help take the offering to the audience.' Numbers, therefore, help the industry get organised, they help the brand make an informed sponsorship choice and help to efficiently reach out to audiences. All this talk of accountability, transparency, ROI and measurability seems to indicate that numbers are more important to the success of an IP than ideas. But it would be a huge mistake to think this way. The truth is that the industry is very comfortable with ideas; it is in evaluation and numbers where most professionals lack. So while both are equally important, there is far more ground to be covered on the business aspect. Vinit firmly says that only numbers will not do. It's all about how numbers can help an idea become larger than life and reach the right people.

THE IPL STORY

The IPL is one of those trendsetting stories that had got it all covered right from the beginning. The packaging was fantastic, the format crisp and engaging and the licensing planned to the T. The colour of team apparels was as much of an event and talking point as the actual league matches. In Vinit Karnik's words, 'Marketing made IPL a success.' He should know, because he and the team were involved in the IPL from the very beginning. Let us start with our first point, measurability. From franchise allocation and player auctions to the launch of the league and matches, everything was a marketed event with numbers carefully documented and then amplified. The format took the consumer along right from the start and made it worth the while for any brand looking for fresh avenues to engage with consumers. The ROI of brands were delivered by the scale and the obviously adoring fan following that lapped up every bit of IPL content on air and online. ROO was delivered for brands that were looking to be salient, to block competition or even focus on specific geographies. From an infrastructure and packaging point of view, constant entertainment, celebrity spotting and live music made the ground event 'un-missable'.

Vinit Karnik helped add perspective with some astounding figures. 'For the first time ever, we saw a sporting league spend between INR 40-50 crore on media to reach out as a brand. That is normally the size of an entire brand campaign. Which sports league has ever done this before the cricket IPL?'

The media plan alone was INR 50-odd crore. For the first time ever, India saw a brand spend INR 40 crore for title sponsorship. INR 40 crore for a 45-day event was pretty much a dream. To sum up the effectiveness of the IPL strategy, Vinit points out, 'IPL reached out to and communicated with the consumer and created events on everything that they did or said.'

Vinit Karnik has a whole lot more up his sleeve, including three-to-five minute short format films with top Bollywood A-listers to cater to the diminishing attention spans of the modern consumer. We will wait for this and lots more from the experiential industry in the next few years.

'IPL reached out to and communicated with the consumer and created events around everything that they did or said.'

EPILOGUE: STAGE WHISPERS

When I first started writing *Staged!,* I had spoken to some people in the know – to understand how the complex world of publishing works, where to start and how best to get what I knew to be a compelling story, across to event professionals and aspirants. At that time, several authors told me that it takes years to write a book, but I couldn't help doubting it a bit. I gave myself the ambitious target of six months to write about the industry that has been taking shape over a quarter of a century. As it turned out, the estimates I had received were right. It's been over two years since I set about writing the story, and it's only now that the book has been published.

Through all this, I must admit that I have learnt as much about events in the two years of writing this book than I have in all my years in the industry. There is a lesson in this somewhere — different event agencies, and their unique propositions are as diverse as consumption palates. For instance, if there is a big enough market for alternative Indian music, then a savvy event manager with a finger on the pulse of that audience, can build a successful practice that primarily creates and offers experiences in this genre. Similarly, there are large and successful event businesses that cater only to corporate events because the proprietor understands the requirements and can add value to it. There are other agencies that specialise in sports, art and culture-based events, weddings, backstage management, employee engagement programmes, promotional events for children and schools etc. Even with a decade or more of experience, event professionals manage to work in just a handful of these genres. Through *Staged!* I have attempted to accomplish two objectives.

First, to isolate those factors common to events across genres and geographies. These are factors that are so integral to events that professionals need to have a working knowledge of them no matter which aspect they specialise in. I see them as the unifying factors of events, which allow agencies to innovate, progress and keep in touch with the demands of the market. Some unifying factors integral to all events are technology, principles of creativity, design thinking, event sponsorship and marketing. To throw light on these core factors, I have spoken to leaders in the field of events, who are exemplary in the way they have used these factors to add value to clients, businesses and the consumer. Their thoughts and views as expressed through this book are invaluable for entrepreneurs considering an events venture, and professionals looking at becoming thought leaders in the industry.

The second objective is to let readers considering a future in events, know the options open to them. There is a reason why students of Communication Management often study the basics for a year or more before they choose a specialisation (in events / public relations / journalism, etc.). Similarly, it is impossible to make an informed decision about the genre or role in events best fit for you, unless you have a working knowledge of everything that is involved. With subjects like event IPs, sports, music, exhibitions and more covered, *Staged!* attempts to facilitate not only the decision of whether to join events, but also which aspect of events is best suited for an individual.

What stood out very strongly across all the interviews I conducted with the leaders in the industry was a very strong work culture and ethic. The Wizcraft directors **Andre Timmins, Sabbas Joseph** and **Viraf Sarkari** are arguably the biggest names in the business. While they can give lessons on practically every aspect of the industry, in *Staged!*, they have spoken about putting Indian events on the global map.

Anil Singh and **Vivek Singh** of Procam International, the premier sports marketing agency, believe strongly that sports should get their due. Besides the Mumbai Marathon that they are most famous for, several of their other successes in creating sporting event properties have been at promoting sports as a culture among consumers. The brothers made sports a comfortable watching experience; they took it to television; they marketed it and they made sports and sports stars household names. Their firm conviction that sports belongs amongst the most engaging and profitable ventures convinced detractors and helped them brave their own setbacks.

When I met **Brian Tellis** of Fountainhead, I discovered that he has a passion for the story behind brands. What probably endears him to his clients is that he scratches beneath the surface to reveal the back-story of regular brands to unearth the story behind them that consumers would really like to know.

Devraj Sanyal of Universal Music Group and EMI Music, is the only successful Managing Director at his level who is actually a musician himself. What sets him entirely apart from other top music honchos is that his keen business acumen is matched only by his appreciation of music.

Martin da Costa of Seventy Event Media Group has succeeded by bringing his international sensibilities to Indian ideas. His measured balance between the two has won him clients, many of whom feel he is the only one who has truly been able to understand both Indian sentiments and global requirements of a project.

One of the senior most industry leaders, **Michael Menezes** of Showtime, has always felt that technology can do a lot to elevate the level of experience that can be offered at live events. He pioneered several technology firsts despite prohibitively expensive logistics in several cases.

Mohomed Morani of Cineyug is behind some of the most glamorous events both on television and on ground. His events are almost like Bollywood production…on stage.

A man who's been a guide and mentor to me, **Roshan Abbas** of Encompass, creates events with the beauty of a theatrical production. Over the few hours that an event plays out on stage, Roshan makes it seem like several acts of a single play, with a unified story connecting it all.

Roshan's partner, **Sukrit Singh** founded and built Encompass with him. He's managed to strike the rare and remarkable balance between strategy and visual creative to stand out as one of the most influential figures in shaping the industry.

Sanjoy K Roy of Teamwork Arts has made it his mission to bring about social change through the arts and culture. This sets him apart from everybody else in the industry. In this book, he talks of his various successes and how he changed the way people think, across different countries.

Exhibition is a large business, and **Sumit Gandhi** and **Manish Gandhi** of ABEC are the biggest indigenous names in the field. What makes them successful is their understanding of business requirements and their ability to create a 'show' of what is essentially a B2B (business-to-business) meeting.

Vijay Nair of OML is the man behind the NH7 Weekender Music Festival, and the face of new-age events. He creates events that have consumers asking for more. What makes him valuable is the pull factor that he manages to create for his event properties.

All creativity comes to naught if we can't make a business of events. **Vinit Karnik** of ESP Properties talks of how he makes business happen with examples from the cricket IPL and more.

The more the world goes virtual, the more real the need for events becomes. In fact, I think the two worlds will meet sooner rather than later, with virtual events being added to the mix. With events poised where they are today, all we know is that the best is yet to be staged!

ACKNOWLEDGEMENTS

Besides the industry leaders who have spoken through the chapters, I want to thank a few people without whom this book would not have been possible.

Too many people said that event management is too niche a topic for general consumption, so a book on it is a risky proposition. But it took just one individual with keen foresight to make the dream a reality. Ajay Mago, Publisher, Om Books International, decided to be the first to take the REAL story of events to the very many who have been fascinated by the industry but had no access to it.

Navneeth Mohan, one of the youngest achievers in the big league in this industry, helped with strategic insights on the direction of the industry.

I also received a patient hearing and actionable direction from one of the keenest minds in publishing, Padmini Mirchandani.

Amrita Sarkar, independent designer, ex-colleague and an old friend has designed the cover of this book to reflect the bustling and lively industry that *Staged!* is about.

Several people read excerpts from the book in advance and shared their excitement and valuable feedback. However, the most insightful suggestions came from Dipa Chaudhuri, Chief Editor, Om Books International; without her direction, this book would not do justice to the readers who have long awaited its release.